Missiological Reflections on Life and Mission

"If you are comfortable with what you believe, you do not want to read this book. The author dives headfirst into contemporary issues relevant to missions and ministry with a stringent realism. . . . At times you may be uncomfortable, but reading this book is well worth the risk. I recommend you do it in company with others."

—**William Phillips**, retired pastor and former missionary to Romania

"Davis provides a wonderful potpourri of missiological and theological reflections by a seasoned cross-cultural practitioner with a lifetime of wisdom and experience. You will find articles in this volume that will cause you to think deeply, engage earnestly, and intensify your commitment to missions . . . . A helpful collection of solid contemplations for those interested in taking the gospel around the world."

—**Jeff Straub**, www.JeffStraub.net

"Davis has stirred up the pond in this book. Topics that have begun to lay dormant are raised for contemporary discussion. He models the importance of balancing the tension between staying true to God's word and humbly exploring the edges of sometimes divisive topics. This book will ease those uncomfortable with these topics into edifying discussions."

—**Ed Scheuerman**, Lancaster Bible College

"No one training for ministry or entering into the pastorate can afford to neglect the key issues Davis wrestles with in this work. No matter where you fall politically or denominationally, Davis presents a solid case to keep the gospel central to the church's mission. Gospel focus will not only lead to the church's much-needed ongoing reform but also equip the church to reach the world effectively with the hope only found in Christ."

—**Andrew Zakhari**, assistant pastor, Stone Hill Church

Missiological Reflections on Life and Mission

Stephen M. Davis

FOREWORD BY
Edward L. Smither

WIPF & STOCK · Eugene, Oregon

MISSIOLOGICAL REFLECTIONS ON LIFE AND MISSION

Copyright © 2022 Stephen M. Davis. All rights reserved. Except for brief quotations in critical publications or reviews, no part of this book may be reproduced in any manner without prior written permission from the publisher. Write: Permissions, Wipf and Stock Publishers, 199 W. 8th Ave., Suite 3, Eugene, OR 97401.

Wipf & Stock
An Imprint of Wipf and Stock Publishers
199 W. 8th Ave., Suite 3
Eugene, OR 97401

www.wipfandstock.com

PAPERBACK ISBN: 978-1-6667-3768-4
HARDCOVER ISBN: 978-1-6667-9740-4
EBOOK ISBN: 978-1-6667-9741-1

05/11/22

Scripture quotations are from the ESV® Bible (The Holy Bible, English Standard Version®), copyright © 2001 by Crossway, a publishing ministry of Good News Publishers. Used by permission. All rights reserved.

Scripture quotations marked (KJV) are taken from The Authorized (King James) Version. Rights in the Authorized Version in the United Kingdom are vested in the Crown. Reproduced by permission of the Crown's patentee, Cambridge University Press.

Dedicated

To those who left hearth and home,

Their supreme desire to make Christ known;

Some to die a martyr's death, to rise again someday,

Some to live and serve in places far away.

Their sacrifice forgotten in human history,

Crown of life, "well done" for eternity.

Contents

Foreword by Edward L. Smither | ix
Preface | xi
Introduction | xv

Chapter 1: The Church's Priorities in Missions | 1
Chapter 2: Good Works and Missions | 7
Chapter 3: Salvation in Christ Alone | 13
Chapter 4: Dreams, Visions, Angelic Visitations | 21
Chapter 5: Do We Need Signs and Wonders in Missions? | 29
Chapter 6: Reflections on the Gospel of the Kingdom | 36
Chapter 7: Poverty Alleviation and the Gospel | 43
Chapter 8: Israel in God's Program for the Church | 50
Chapter 9: Is Allah the Father of Jesus? | 58
Chapter 10: Music, Worship, and Missions | 63
Chapter 11: Agreeing to Walk and Minister Together | 69
Chapter 12: The Gospel and Multi-Ethnicity | 75
Chapter 13: Monocultural Myopia | 81
Chapter 14: African Traditional Religion | 87
Chapter 15: Polygamy in Africa | 93
Chapter 16: Community and Individualism in the Church | 102
Conclusion: A Final Plea for Missional Living | 110

Bibliography | 119

Foreword

FROM TIME TO TIME, I will connect with a veteran missionary, pastor, or theologian and I'm eager to learn more about their journey. What's the craziest thing they've ever encountered in ministry? What key life lessons have they learned that they would like to pass on? What would they have done differently? For some people, not knowing where to begin, such questions can be overwhelming. I have some friends that do life histories with veteran missionaries and missiologists—publishing them as short articles or even podcasts—in order to preserve their stories and gain from their wisdom.

Steve Davis and his wife Kathy have had a wonderful journey in mission—from planting a church in Philadelphia, to serving cross-culturally in Romania and France, and then back to Philadelphia for more pastoral ministry as well as working as an addictions counselor. Steve's doctoral studies took him to Columbia International University (where we met) where he put together a fantastic study on secularization in France and its missiological implications. So Steve Davis is someone I would want to have coffee or a meal with and hear his stories and what he has learned in mission.

In this book, that is exactly what Steve has done for us. Framing the book with some critical missiological questions, Steve offers wisdom to younger missionaries and pastors starting on their journey. Some of the questions are more theological: Is salvation in Christ alone? What is the Gospel of the Kingdom? Where does Israel fit in the Church's program? Other questions arise from the missionary encounter: How do we deal with dreams, visions, and angelic visitations? Are Allah and the Father of Jesus the same person? What do African traditional religions teach? Some questions really raise the practical realities of living and making disciples across cultures: What do we do about polygamy? What are the differences between communal and individual cultures?

The breadth of the questions in this book show that Steve has served in some very different contexts in Europe and Africa, and he has taken time to process these questions with biblical and theological reflection. Steve has been a committed practitioner serving in mission at the street level for decades; but he is also an astute theological and missiological thinker. He has labored faithfully and reflected deeply. And the reader gets to benefit from both values.

This book would be helpful for different types of people: those training for global mission in a college or seminary; young missionaries starting out in ministry in the European or African context; as well as other veteran missionaries who also need a model for how to tell their stories. I commend this book and pray we will learn from Steve Davis's wisdom in his journey in mission.

Edward L. Smither, PhD

Dean, College of Intercultural Studies
Columbia International University

Preface

OUR TIMES ARE IN the Lord's hands (Ps 31:15). "All must come, and last, and end, As shall please my heavenly Friend."[1] Over forty years of ministry have passed. All I can say is that I am still amazed that God saved me, transformed my life, and has allowed me to serve him. I am originally from Philadelphia and spent my earliest years in a Philadelphia housing project in the East Falls section of Philadelphia. When I was young we moved from the projects to a rowhouse in the Feltonville section of the city where I shared a bedroom with my four brothers, the fifth brother coming some years later. Since there were only two sisters they had their own bedroom. We were by no means well-to-do but never considered ourselves poor. My dad worked three jobs, his main job as a prison guard for the city prison system. At the age of seventeen, I dropped out of high school and was usually on the wrong side of the law. My brother John became a Christian in 1970 and for three years hounded me about "getting saved." In December 1973, God won the battle going on in my life and I surrendered. After my conversion I left the city for Chicago to get away from the drug culture, the police, and from anyone looking for me to settle scores. I lived with Pastor William Schroeder and his family for nine formative months before going to Bob Jones University from 1974 to 1978 and married my wife Kathy shortly after graduation.

---

1. "Sovereign Ruler of the Skies," ©Public Domain.

PREFACE

In 1982, after four years of seminary, much to my surprise we went to Philadelphia to start a church in Roxborough in Northwest Philadelphia. After that church was established, I left the city again with my family in January 1988, this time for ministry in France and then Romania, before returning to the United States in 1998 to pursue doctoral studies under missiologists such as David Hesselgrave, Paul Hiebert, and Tite Tiénou at Trinity Evangelical Divinity School. For several years, as director of missions of Calvary Baptist Church in Lansdale, PA, I travelled and taught widely in Asia, the Middle East, Africa, and South America. From 2006 to 2008 my wife and I were back in France to work with a Paris church without a pastor and we helped plant a new church in the Paris suburbs. We returned to Philadelphia in 2009 to plant a church with my brother John and his wife Dawn. For several years I worked bi-vocationally as an addiction therapist and have had the privilege of doing pastoral training in Yaoundé, Cameroon twice a year.

If my cross-cultural ministry experiences have not been deep, they have at least been broad. I've learned some things along the way and am still trying to figure out some others. Besides living for several years overseas in France and Romania, my travels have taken me to interesting places at unusual times. In June 1981 I was in Israel for a study trip when the Israeli Air Force bombed an unfinished Iraqi nuclear reactor near Baghdad. Our group was blissfully unaware of the attack, but our families back home feared retaliation on Israel while we were still there. In August 1995 I was leading a vision trip for American college students through several countries after the breakup of Yugoslavia. NATO commenced Operation Deliberate Force in targeted areas around Sarajevo. We were in a safe zone but former US miliary men in our group sensed ground vibrations and suspected something was not right. Not knowing exactly what was going on, we made a mad dash north for the Hungarian border. A Serbian pastor friend siphoned gas from his vehicle since there was none available at service stations. On the way to Hungary, we had our passports taken by the police at a toll booth and couldn't leave until we paid an exorbitant amount of money in American dollars and Deutsch marks. Once in Hungary we discovered what had happened and were grateful for God's providential care. I was in China in 2002 during the SARS outbreak. We took a train from Shenzhen to Hong Kong and wondered why everyone was wearing masks. We soon discovered why and my family worried I'd be quarantined upon my return. In July 2006 I had an extended layover in Paris on my way to Beirut for a church building dedication service. Israel had bombed Hezbollah military targets and Lebanese civilian infrastructure including Rafic Hariri International Airport in Beirut and I had to return home. During another teaching trip to Lebanon I took a taxi from Beirut to Damascus with two Lebanese Christians and an American friend to visit Christian Iraqi refugees from Mosul. After the fall of communism, God gave me the opportunity to preach at a church in Moscow that was meeting in a building that had been used by the KGB to hold prisoners. I had dinner in Beijing with a high-level Chinese official who was concerned about his daughter who became a Christian while studying nursing at a Christian college in the United States. He thought she had joined a cult and we were able to speak to him about the gospel.

My experiences and training have changed me and challenged me. This book represents my thinking in some areas of Christian missions. The Great Commission given by our risen Savior has never changed. What changes are the times, the opportunities, the challenges, and our perspectives. My confidence in myself and my own abilities has decreased over the years. My confidence in the authority of God's word continues to grow. Like all Christians, I want to hear those words "well done" from the Savior and I would like to be remembered as a faithful man, although no one will remember me as a perfect man. My salvation from beginning to end is one of grace. God saved me and promised to keep me, promised to complete the work he began. Apart from him and his power to keep me until my entrance into his eternal kingdom, I would have no hope. These years in ministry have been nothing if not interesting. When I was running the streets of Philly, no one could have imagined that I would still be alive today, much less serving the Lord. I have never been accused of being humble. Yet I know that any accomplishments, any ministry, any investment in the lives of others would have been impossible without a mighty God at work in my life and his good gifts to me. For all that I am and will be eternally grateful.

Introduction

ONE OF THE GREAT missiological questions of our day concerns the mission of the church in a world that has largely been evangelized. By that I do not mean, of course, that every nation, tribe, and language has been reached with the gospel or that every person alive at any time in history had access to hearing the gospel. We know that there are millions of people today who have not yet heard the gospel. The apostle Paul in his day spoke of the gospel bearing fruit "in the whole world" and "proclaimed in all creation under heaven" (Col 1:6, 23). We can speak in the same way in our day. One hundred years ago only slightly more than 5 percent of non-Christians personally knew a Christian and over half the world's population was unevangelized. Today 18 percent of non-Christians personally know a follower of Jesus and the number of those unevangelized has fallen to 28 percent.[1]

So the days are largely gone when the West sent missionaries to unknown lands and people. Apart from isolated ethnic peoples in yet unreached regions and limited access nations, the gospel has essentially been preached worldwide and Christianity thrives in places where a century ago Christians were few and far between. This can be seen especially in the shift of Christianity from Europe and North America to South America, Africa, and Asia. Current trends show that Christianity continues to expand globally with

1. Earls, "Encouraging Trends," para. 5.

charismatics and evangelicals the two fastest growing groups.[2] In addition, contact between ethnic groups, whether resulting from immigration, warfare and displacement, or tourism is unprecedented. Times have changed. We have more opportunities, more resources and are the benefactors of more past experience and research than any previous generation.

As Christians continue taking the gospel cross-culturally we need to better understand other cultures and reject any notion of cultural superiority. Please understand that this assertion in no way diminishes the impact and contribution of different cultures. We are cultural beings. It is impossible to separate our expression of Christianity from our culture. Yet Christianity is a universal religion not bound by one cultural expression of it. It is unavoidable that western churches have a certain flavor that reflects elements of culture, for example, in liturgy, in architecture, in church government, and in discipleship. However one should not expect that cultural aspects be reproduced in churches planted among other peoples. Other cultures, although in need of transformation, are adequate, albeit imperfect, socio-cultural environments in which the gospel can take root. No cultural way of life or its Christian expression should be absolutized. Yet cultures are free to borrow from other cultures and incorporate change into their culture.

During my visits to Africa I noticed that many pastor friends wore western dress suits in city churches and traditional dress in village churches. For special events they wore robes which were reminiscent of eighteenth-century European Anglican missionaries. They are not bound to wear those robes; they are free to wear them. When we graduated our first cohort of pastors in Cameroon, they requested a graduation ceremony like those they had seen in videos in the West. So we ordered gowns for the graduates complete with mortarboard cap and tassel. I wore my distinguished looking doctoral gown and sweated throughout the ceremony. We accommodated their request, gave them certificates and MacArthur Study Bibles in French, and had a glorious time with graduates and their families.

2. Earls, "Encouraging Trends," para. 2.

INTRODUCTION

We must not, however, impose our culture on those we partner with or seek to reach for Christ, leading to cultural conversions that prevent new churches from taking root in their cultural milieu. Obviously those elements in any culture which are clearly contradictory to Scripture must be abandoned. Yet a refusal to allow for cultural variables may attract mostly those who are disenchanted with their own culture and way of life. Converts might embrace Western Christianity in order to receive not only salvation but also the "cargo" of Christianity. Without cross-cultural training missionaries may unconsciously confound their cultural expression of Christianity with biblical absolutes or supracultural truth.[3] As an example, I remember vividly during our years in France how American missionaries would preach against wine, not simply against drunkenness and advocating moderation as the Bible teaches, but drinking wine at all. Although I have no problem with a total abstinence position from a personal wisdom standpoint, to preach against wine in France betrays a misunderstanding of the Bible and French culture. Of course I do not advocate absolute relativism which postulates that no absolute standards exist outside of culture, or ethical relativism that insists that practices which exist in other cultures should receive approval merely because they serve a purpose in that culture. All cultures and cultural practices must be examined under the light of the word of God.

Missionaries should have strong convictions but they will be confronted with countless challenges to their own worldview assumptions. They must also learn to distinguish between ontological convictions rooted in Scripture and culture-informed convictions. In other words, they must be willing to learn and to change as led by God's word and Spirit. Missionaries risk emphasizing areas of conscience informed by cultural variables in their home culture which find no resonance in the conscience of the host culture. This may lead to surface conformity, where believers remain deeply attached in their worldview commitments to their pre-Christian allegiances. Just as first-century cultural Gentiles were not required to become cultural Jews in

3. Hesselgrave, *Communicating Christ*, 103–4.

order to convert (i.e., circumcision and law-keeping), we must not present conversion as a break from culture per se but only from those elements found in all cultures that are incompatible with revealed truth and kingdom living.

In the following chapters I want to address some missiological challenges I've faced in over forty years of ministry in my home culture and cross-culturally. Some of the issues would never have come to my attention without exposure to other cultures. I don't pretend that others will face the same challenges or respond in the same way. What we need is the ability to reflect biblically, theologically, and missiologically on whatever issues we face, and we need the conviction that God is at work in his world to accomplish his purposes and bring all things to his desired end.

Chapter 1

The Church's Priorities in Missions

THE CHANGING FACE OF world missions presents unique challenges and has rearranged the church's priorities. Although there are areas in which our thinking must change in order to meet the challenges inherent in cross-cultural gospel ministry, we must resist cultural and sociological pressure to minimize biblical priorities. There is considerable debate on the mission of the church, both from within the broad parameters of Protestant, Orthodox, and Roman Catholic traditions,[1] and within broader Evangelicalism.[2] Some expand the mission of the church as does Christopher Wright who delineates three domains of an expanded mission: cultivating the church, engaging society, and caring for creation.[3] My own view aligns more with Jonathan Leeman's in seeing the church's priority "to make disciples by declaring or mediating God's judgment" in light of the truth that "the threat of God's eternal wrath is the most urgent of all."[4] There are several words used to describe the church's mission. There is also confusion about their meaning since these words are not found in the New Testament. Definitions do matter and we often see that "an uncritical use of words, and in particular a lack of shared definition for the words mission, missions, missionary, and missional,

1. See Bevans et al, *Mission of the Church*.
2. See Leeman et al, *Four Views*.
3. C. J. H. Wright, "Participatory Mission," 81.
4. Leeman, "Soteriological Mission," 29–30.

has led to a distortion of Jesus' biblical mandate. . . ."[5] When I speak of "missions" in the plural, I am distinguishing it from what we might understand as the "mission" of the church in the singular. The mission of the church is broader than missions and includes more than missions, the latter generally understood as "that part of the mission of the Church that seeks to cross cultural, religious, and ethnic boundaries to introduce and further the work of the gospel."[6] Of course, as Köstenberger states, "the cross-cultural aspect of Christian ministry is not a necessary part of mission. To be sure, mission may, and frequently will, involve the crossing of ethnic, cultural, or other boundaries, but this is not an integral part of the New Testament concept of mission itself."[7]

This changing face of world missions has led to a shift in many circles from gospel proclamation and church planting to more engagement in humanitarian work. I have no problem with seeing humanitarian work as part of the mission of any particular church who feels called and has the resources to engage in it. Whose heart doesn't ache seeing people in misery? Our own local church seeks to bless our community in doing good because we are Christians and are commanded to love our neighbors as ourselves (Mark 12:31). Sometimes doors for gospel witness are opened; sometimes not. As John Piper has often stated, "We care about all suffering now, especially eternal suffering later."[8] One problem I see, however, is that "we now live in a time when the Church thinks of itself as doing missions even if the gospel is never shared."[9] For others, including myself, gospel proclamation remains the church's priority in missions with the intent to plant churches. True, fewer foreign resident missionaries might be needed in some places and roles might shift from pioneer church planting to training leadership in places where Christianity has made great advances. We might need to regularly and prayerfully

---

5. Spitters and Ellison, *Everything is Missions*, 22–23.
6. Corwin, "MissionS," 72.
7. Köstenberger, "Place of Mission," 347–48.
8. Piper, "Suffering," para. 6.
9. Payne, "Currents of Change," 11.

rethink strategy, use of resources, and mission models, but the church's unique message and engagement in world missions continue unchanged until the return of Christ.

As I understand the New Testament, churches are the fruit and goal of evangelism and discipleship. Our missionary engagement must intentionally focus on preaching the gospel, making disciples, and gathering believers in worshipping communities which follow biblical doctrine and standards, yet churches which reflect in some measure their culture. Churches that are truly indigenous "look different from location to location. Further, they look different from generation to generation."[10] Yet, as Bosch observes, historically "young churches 'planted' on the 'mission fields' were replicas of the churches on the mission agency's home front."[11] With hindsight we usually see the errors of those who preceded us more clearly than our own. We should, however, be generous toward our mission forerunners. In time, others will see our errors. Yet Bosch's observation is well taken. One lamentable result of past and present mission practices is that many of these churches failed to reproduce in their culture because of their foreignness. Of course, all churches are foreign in some respects and in all places, but with a foreignness which comes from the Bible not from another earthly culture.

A priority on church planting in missions refuses to accept a detrimental enlargement or redefinition of the mission of the church where gospel proclamation and making disciples becomes secondary to local issues or social agenda, and where errors of the past are used to justify mission shifts which lack biblical support. For example, Bosch, who offers great insights in many areas, regrettably enlarges "the church's missionary engagement in respect of the realities of injustice, oppression, poverty, discrimination, and violence."[12] These are important concerns and cannot be ignored. These concerns, however, are best addressed by individual Christians working for change in their communities through their civic

10. Stetzer, *Missional Churches*, 31.
11. Bosch, *Transforming Mission*, 5.
12. Bosch, *Transforming Mission*, 10.

responsibilities. They are also addressed by the church through the transformation of lives rather than through a social agenda as part of the church's missionary engagement. David Hesselgrave wrote that if we are not clear in how we understand the mission of the church and our engagement in missions, "we surrender the distinctive priorities of the Christian mission and risk assignment of the word to the terminological dustbin."[13] I also agree that "when everything is missions, some of the most central aspects may be lost or buried—such as sending our own to make disciples and plant churches cross-culturally."[14]

My concern is mission drift where the essential is buried and lost in extending the church's mission to engage in worthy causes or in redefining the mission. For example, one author admonishes Christians to accept "reconciliation as the necessary paradigm of mission in the age of unprecedented global fragmentation."[15] Advocates of this new and necessary paradigm recognize the past efforts by "courageous evangelicals who dared to challenge myopic evangelism-only missiology" and "sought to reintegrate social justice into the evangelical missionary agenda."[16] This newly-discovered reconciliation paradigm now calls the church to move beyond mere word and deed ministry. The pressing need is to "advance the meaning of holistic mission, to build on the evangelism and social justice affirmation." How is this done? By "joining God in *putting the world back together again*. It needs to be about participating with God in the healing of the nations."[17] I'm not sure I know what that means, and even if I did, how to do it. Far from me to argue against the necessity of reconciliation which has always been an integral part of gospel proclamation, reconciling sinners to God and the implication of reconciliation between people. Paul tells us in 2 Cor 5:15–19, "All this is from God, who through Christ reconciled us to himself and gave us the ministry of reconciliation; that is,

---

13. Hesselgrave, *Communicating Christ*, 3.
14. Spitters and Ellison, *Everything is Missions*, 20.
15. Tizon, *Whole and Reconciled*, xvi.
16 Tizon, *Whole and Reconciled*, xvii.
17. Tizon, *Whole and Reconciled*, xvii.

in Christ God was reconciling the world to himself, not counting their trespasses against them, and entrusting to us the message of reconciliation." The healing *of* the nations mentioned above should be called healing *within* the nations. Today the nations rage against the Lord and his anointed and are called to embrace Christ (Ps 2:2, 12). I have no expectation for the healing of the nations apart from divine intervention in the millennium or new heaven and new earth (Isa 2:4, 11:6–9; Rev 21:2; 22:2). We are presently participating with God in reconciliation through transformation brought about by the gospel. In this age, reconciliation takes place as men and women are reconciled to God. I'm also skeptical about "myopic evangelism-only missiology," which might have existed in some form, but sounds more like a straw man. If it's code for the priority of gospel proclamation, however, count me in.

For several decades there have been calls for a "missionary moratorium" coming from national church leaders in countries which have long had a missionary presence and who believe it is time for churches to find their own identity. In some places these calls are a reflection of anti-American sentiments and historical grievances connected to colonialism and the dominance exercised by Western mission agencies.[18] They might also be a reflection of mainline churches who feel threatened by evangelical missions. I do not support a missionary moratorium. We do, however, need to think more strategically about partnerships with national churches to serve them and their needs, especially the need for theological education. Further, in my opinion, most Western church planters should not be lead pastors of churches if there are nationals to work with from the start. I believe this subordination of nationals is one reason lying behind the call for a missionary moratorium.

Truly pioneer situations exist where there are no qualified believers for leadership and which may require a missionary-church planter to assume the role of pastor. There are also times when missionaries enter a vacuum and start from scratch with years dedicated to Bible translation before any effective evangelism and discipling can take place. Yet there are many places where churches

---

18. Tizon, "Moratorium Debate," 13.

have existed for decades in which a foreigner remains as lead pastor with national assistants. When his ministry comes to an end for whatever reason, he is replaced by another missionary. I have been in situations where I had no choice and needed to be the lead pastor in a foreign country. I have experienced other times where I was able to be part of a team with nationals and not be at the forefront. Whenever possible I prefer teamwork and playing a supporting role alongside nationals rather than leading them with no end in sight.

I can't tell you how many missionaries have left home with great expectations of church planting on foreign soil with no idea of how to enter the culture, how to plant a church, how to train leadership, and with no exit strategy. They labored for years with little or nothing to show for it and left the field without leaving anything behind. Or they stayed on the field well beyond their usefulness. Now I do understand that there are times of sowing seed without results like Adoniram Judson and others who labored for years without visible fruit in pioneer situations. There are no guarantees of what might be called successful ministry. In our time most of those leaving the United States to plant churches elsewhere have the opportunity to partner with nationals and work as a team. And if church planters aren't really planting churches then something needs to change. As a balance to the "missionary mantra of late [which] has been 'Work yourself out of a job,' one has to wonder if a more appropriate goal would be, 'Build something that lasts.'"[19]

If we lose the priority of evangelism, discipleship, and church planting, and we attach "missions" to our evangelism-free projects, we should not be surprised by the slow advance of the gospel. If what we are doing and calling missions is in reality good works indistinguishable from the good works done by non-Christian organizations, then we should question whether we should at least call these endeavors something else. If what we are doing is good, commendable, and needed good works, yet there is no intentionality in telling people about Jesus, there is no gospel, and there is no offense of the cross, then let's reevaluate our commitment to the Great Commission.

19. Clark, *Mission Affirmed*, 21.

―― Chapter 2 ――

Good Works and Missions

THE LAST CHAPTER'S EMPHASIS on the priority of evangelism and church planting does not minimize the place and importance of good works for which we are created in Christ Jesus (Eph 2:10). There is much to be commended in doing good works, and we are not heartless toward poverty, injustice, and oppression. My disagreement with present trends is not that churches are doing good works in imitation of Jesus who "went about doing good" (Acts 10:38). I'm simply asking if they are also doing what God clearly and pointedly commanded them to do. Churches need to understand the culture where they serve and are free to engage their own communities in ways that best serve God's purposes as they understand them. Recently there has been a wave of Afghan immigrants after the debacle ending the war in Afghanistan. Churches have risen to the occasion to provide shelter, food, and ESL classes. These efforts may or may not lead to opportunities for gospel witness, especially with the language barrier. Whether evangelism takes place or not, they are good works and reflect the love and compassion of God's people. Sadly, there are churches which no longer preach the gospel and good works are their main ministry because they have nothing else to offer. Local churches can do a great deal in their communities to build bridges and gain a hearing for the gospel. We often have people coming off the street during or after our services requesting food. They are not yet at a place where they are ready to gather with Christians. We would not deny them a cup of water in

Jesus' name (Mark 9:41). In doing good works, however, we must not neglect what God has actually commanded the church to do—make disciples of all the nations!

More specifically, when we consider the place of good works in cross-cultural ministry, the focus of our efforts must remain gospel proclamation and church planting. It is possible for well-meaning mission endeavors to address social issues as a priority. Short-term needs are met but seeds are sown for unhealthy dependency. It also makes planting indigenous churches difficult if outside funds are required for every aspect of ministry. Structures are created—schools, orphanages, clinics, camps—which often are not only inadequate for meeting long-term needs, but they also distract from the essential task of planting reproductive fellowships of believers. These good works are not essential to the missionary task nor mandated by the word of God. They are laudable and may open doors for the gospel and in certain contexts may be required for entrance into some countries. I have a missionary friend who could not enter his country of ministry for church planting without opening and operating an orphanage. He had no choice in the matter and the orphanage was a good work. He also experienced what others have experienced in creating foreigner-dependent orphanages—an influx of "orphans" sent by their parents to have a better life than what the parents could provide. Missionaries will have to decide whether to accept the strictures imposed on them.

In my opinion, as much as possible, additional church programs and institutions should be developed which are at least partially supported financially by new churches in keeping with their means. This does not preclude strategic partnership or sharing abundant resources with those less well-endowed. But if these ministries are not part of the vision of national churches and under the auspices of local churches then they effectively remain parachurch ministries and are likely destined for perpetual dependency or failure. The cycle of dependency is extremely difficult to break. And as Glenn Schwartz wisely observes, "When outside money and other material things accompany the spread of the Christian Gospel, sometimes people get the wrong impression about the Gospel itself."[1]

The COVID-19 pandemic has had mostly nefarious global effects. If anything good has come out of the travel restrictions and lockdowns, it is that many ministries stateside have had to rethink their strategies and many of our brothers and sisters in Christ have carried on the work without depending on their foreign counterparts. Perhaps genuine partnership will be one of the positive outcomes, and ministries which follow church planting will be carried out with more consideration of the cultural and economic realities of the new churches. Recently I had a conversation with a friend who has trained pastors in many foreign contexts. In one country he and his agency labored for years. Their constant investment drained their resources to the point where they wisely needed to pull out of the country. As a result, the nationals continued the work, and the training ministry continues today mostly with local resources and teachers. He told me that leaving that country was the best thing for the churches there.

Of course, there are missionaries who are engaged on multiple fronts in cross-cultural ministry—starting churches, training leadership, business as missions, operating camps, schools, and orphanages. Not all missionaries are called to pioneer church planting ministry and the importance of team ministry cannot be overstated. But if ministry is divorced from evangelism and discipleship in the context of church planting, if missionaries remain in place because it's easier than moving on to needier places, or if church planting missionaries remain with one church for a lifetime of ministry, we should at least raise some serious questions and objections about mission strategy. From a human standpoint, the unreached remain unreached partly because missionaries often go to the same places others have gone to for decades and stay too long in places that have been evangelized and where churches have been planted. Rather than redirect resources and personnel to other fields, new ministries are developed with an increased demand for outside support and new missionaries. Should we ordain men and commit

1. Schwartz, "Cure?," para. 13.

our churches to support them as camp directors, schoolteachers, college and seminary professors, medical personnel, orphanage workers, and then call them missionaries because of geographical displacement? Perhaps there are no easy answers to this question, but we would be unwise to not raise the question.

Although we have vast resources in American churches, they are not unlimited. We must wisely consider how we use those resources. Years ago I was on the board of a foundation which directed funds to help build church buildings. The foundation was created by a wealthy businessman and accomplished much good. I made recommendations for several places outside the United States where I felt the cost of construction for a church building was out of reach for the local community. Through these experiences I've learned that without clarity on building plans and accountability for the funds provided, many projects become a black hole with spiraling costs which are beyond the means of the local congregations. In several places I was shocked by the design and cost of the buildings, made possible only because of outside funds. What aggravated the problem was that local congregations could not afford the maintenance on the buildings and made appeals for more funds from churches in the United States. Often, once church buildings were constructed, pleas for assistance continued for additional projects or repairs.

Of course, there is much to be said for the ongoing edification of churches planted by missionaries as evidenced by the apostle Paul's remaining in a nurturing relationship with churches he planted to bring them to maturity. We see throughout his epistles "his concern for the corporate life of believers."[2] Yet great care must be exercised to bring churches to maturity without creating lifelong dependency which inhibits the reproduction of new churches. I do not propose a grand strategy for how to do that in all places. But more thought needs to be given to both entrance and exit strategy. The first is often emphasized to the neglect of the second. As Steffen points out, "church planters who leave prematurely may harm the church. But they can also harm

2. Peterson, "Goal of Missions," 195.

it by staying too long."³ He proposes a "phase-out oriented model [which] avoids the errors of colonialism by starting partnership very early in the church planting process."⁴

We should be willing to help our brothers and sisters in Christ around the world with our plentiful resources. I encourage generosity and wise investment. There are, however, some practices I consider unwise as presently carried out. For example, there are regular appeals from individuals, churches, and schools for "missions trips" to send "missionaries" to far-flung places to minister to those to whom they cannot speak without an interpreter, to build relationships with those they will never see again, and to do for others what they often can or should do for themselves. I've known churches that send their youth groups to Mexico or other Spanish-speaking countries to work in camps or children's ministry and yet won't send them a half hour away to minister to populations of Spanish speakers at their doorstep. I don't want to sound uncharitable, but what seems to be most important is the experience of the mission tourist. What appears to be missing is asking about outcomes for the recipients of mission trips and whether the hosts were confirmed more deeply in their dependence on naively generous Americans. Attaching "mission" to almost any word is the key even if there is never any contact with unbelievers with the gospel. D. A. Carson relates his experience with groups claiming to do holistic ministry in Chicago with the poor or digging wells in foreign deserts "even though few if any of the workers have taken the time to explain to anyone who Jesus is and what he has done to reconcile us to God. Their ministry isn't holistic. It's halfistic, or quarteristic."⁵

I remember well one mission trip where church members were sent to another country to paint buildings at a seminary. Seminary students came to watch and thanked the Americans for their ministry. I couldn't help but thinking, Why are we even here? I question the wisdom of spending thousands of dollars on travel

---

3. Steffen, *Passing the Baton*, 13.
4. Steffen, *Passing the Baton*, 25.
5. Carson, "Work for Justice," para. 1.

and accommodations in order to do what others could and should do for themselves. And I wondered how many local painters were deprived of work because Americans came and did it for free. It would be too much to say that no good is accomplished by these trips and that no lives are touched. Short-term mission trips have been a blessing to both the participants and the recipients. There is an undefinable impact made. There is bonding that takes place among participants and young people often return home with more gratitude after having seen conditions in other countries. Some may even sense a call to full-time missionary service. That's all well and good. My question is simply whether there was intentionality in evangelism along with whatever project was planned. Thankfully there's research being done to try to measure the benefits of short-term mission trips and to provide guidance for making them more gospel-centered than participant-centered.[6]

Let's continue to do good works! Let's be wise in the use of our resources! Let's not fail to proclaim the gospel and make disciples!

---

6. See Priest, *Effective Engagement.*

―― Chapter 3 ――

Salvation in Christ Alone

SOME MIGHT FRAME THE title of this chapter as a question. For me, there is no question that the Bible teaches salvation by grace alone in Christ alone by faith alone (Eph 2:8–9). That affirmation does not relieve us from the need to examine not only what we believe but why, and at the same time try to understand why others believe differently. We also have to wrestle with questions concerning those who lived before Christ and without the knowledge we now have on this side of the cross, and those today who never hear the gospel and die without an opportunity to exercise saving faith in Christ. When we think deeply about it, it's not improbable that the majority of people who have ever lived and who are alive today have never clearly heard the gospel. For some this creates great anxiety and understandably so. The main responses to this dilemma are exclusivism, inclusivism, and pluralism.[1] In exclusivism (particularism), one must exercise conscious, personal faith in Christ to be saved; in inclusivism, salvation is possible for some who do not personally hear the gospel and trust Christ as Savior, but they believe in God based on the knowledge of God received in general revelation; in pluralism, salvation is found in other religions. Jesus remains the unique way of salvation for Christians, but not the only way of access to the Father. Often associated with religious pluralism is universalism, which

---

1. Okholm and Phillips, *Four Views on Salvation*, 14–20.

postulates that everyone will eventually be saved or annihilated since there is no eternal punishment.

While we should reflect on the destiny of those we've never known, those who had no opportunity to hear the gospel, our greater concern should be for our neighbor or co-worker who has yet to hear the gospel from us. The writers of the New Testament do not seem as preoccupied by the fate of those outside their evangelistic reach as many are today. They were greatly concerned with making Christ known to all which should be our burden. Still, we wonder if all those who have never heard the gospel, through no fault of their own, including those who lived before the time of Christ, are without hope and without God. Even when we speak of "hearing the gospel" we have to consider Old Testament believers who were saved, as Abraham who "believed the LORD, and he counted it to him as righteousness" (Gen 15:6; Rom 4:3). We will not solve the debate about how much Abraham knew concerning Christ, the cross, and the resurrection. What we do know is that he knew enough to be justified by faith (Rom 4:5) and also that "the faith structures of the Old Testament always anticipated Jesus."[2] We are also told that God "preached the gospel" to Abraham, "the man of faith" (Gal 3:8–9).

We know there were people before Christ's coming who were saved by Christ's sacrifice on the cross without full knowledge of it. The question is whether there are those in our day, deficient in their understanding of the gospel, who are in a similar situation as Abraham. Many Christians who believe that salvation is in Christ alone make allowances for infants and for those who die before an age of accountability, and for the mentally handicapped who appear unable to comprehend their need of a Savior. Many have attempted to resolve this apparent dilemma in different ways. Some would have us believe that God will send someone with the gospel to those he knew beforehand would respond in belief. Others believe that those who never heard the gospel

---

2. Pratt, "Reformed Perspective," 171.

during their lifetime will have an opportunity after death, not a second chance, but a first chance to respond.[3]

Christianity was born in a world of religious pluralism. It has always wrestled with men's and women's souls against religious ideologies. Throughout the centuries the church of Jesus Christ has proclaimed that there is salvation in no other name than in the Lord Jesus Christ (Acts 4:12), and that God works redemptively "through His children's missionary activity to a lost world."[4] There have always been forces at work from outside Christianity to undermine this claim. This central truth, however, has been called into question with a renewed vigor in our day. What has changed is that many of the attacks come from those within professing Christianity. Of course, when we speak of Christianity, "we must insist that religion in itself—even Christianity–is *never* the means of salvation. . . ."[5] The cross of Christ revealed our need of a Savior from sin, our helplessness to save ourselves, the love of God, and the need for grace which alone saves. The biblical position of salvation in Christ alone is being increasingly marginalized; its advocates are treated as intolerant, unscholarly, and unacceptable to the modern mind and scholarly consensus.

The Bible affirms unequivocally that salvation is in Christ alone and that God reveals himself redemptively as the church carries out its mission to preach the gospel. Historically this view has been understood to mean that "only those who hear the gospel of Jesus Christ and explicitly trust in him in this life can be saved, while all others are swept into a lost eternity."[6] There are some evangelical scholars with more nuance who allow that "except perhaps in very special circumstances, people are not saved apart from explicit faith in Jesus Christ."[7] Those special circumstances are not clear and leave room for God to work in extraordinary ways to bring people to a saving knowledge of Christ.

3. See Beilby, *Postmortem Opportunity*.
4. Lindsell, *Christian Philosophy of Missions*, 117.
5. Norman, *Christianity and World Religions*, 30.
6. Okholm and Phillips, *Four Views on Salvation*, 19.
7. Geivett and Phillips, "Evidentialist Approach," 214.

Other evangelicals advocate agnosticism concerning the fate of those who have never had the opportunity to hear the gospel. They are open to the possibility of God working apart from his normal, established means. Alister McGrath asks,

> So what about those who have never heard the gospel? Is the universality of the gospel compromised by the fact that, as a matter of history, the gospel has not been preached to all and its benefits made universally available? . . . A human failure to evangelize cannot be transposed into God's failure to save.[8]

These disagreements among evangelicals will not be resolved and in spite of differences there is a commitment to preaching the gospel of Jesus Christ so that all might hear. What is more concerning are the positions of universalism and religious pluralism which depart from the biblical claim of the absolute uniqueness of Jesus Christ and the indispensability of the new birth. Some of this change might be attributed to globalizing factors. It seemed easier in the past to make pronouncements about the fate of those who were far off and unknown. Many religions which were once far off have now drawn near. The practitioners of these religions are now our neighbors, sincere in their beliefs, and genuinely nice people. We converse with them, dine with them, and our children play together. So the question is asked: Are virtuous Hindus, Buddhists, and Muslims "safe" in their belief systems? Political correctness and religious pluralism answer with a resounding "Yes!" The Bible provides another answer.

We need to be aware of the challenges we face in remaining committed to the authority of Scripture, an authority increasingly denied by many. These challenges are cloaked in deep philosophical speculations and the denial of universal, supracultural, biblical authority. The proponents are well-informed scholars with broad experience in other cultures and religions. Their religious pluralism is connected to an attack on biblical authority and Christological particularism even if they seek scriptural support for their

---

8. McGrath, "Post-Enlightenment Approach," 178.

views. For example, universalists have taken the affirmation that all things in heaven and earth will be united in Christ (Eph 1:10) to support their assertion of universal salvation. We are also told that knowing objective and absolute truth is impossible, and the modern historical consciousness must affirm that all truth claims are culturally conditioned. This posture leads to the criticism that "the tendencies toward absoluteness and exclusivity in traditional Christian faith easily lead to a kind of idolatry that makes it difficult to take other faiths seriously in their own terms."[9] Thus the abandonment of any possibility of knowing absolute religious truth. This epistemological skepticism must make way for the relative validity of all truth claims and paint as arrogant any exclusive claim. The acceptance of the privileged perspective of the modern historical consciousness subtly leads away from a Christocentric view (no salvation apart from Christ) to a theocentric view (no salvation apart from God), and finally to a soteriocentric view that redefines salvation in a sociological context.[10]

J. Oswald Sanders recognized the danger of universalism. He stated,

> The creeping paralysis of universalism—the belief that ultimately all men will be saved—is rapidly gaining ground throughout Christendom. . . . This dangerous doctrine, which minimizes the seriousness of sin, impugns the righteousness of God, emasculates the doctrine of the atonement and denies final judgment, finds no support in Scripture.[11]

He further described universalism as the view that "Christ had already redeemed the whole world, and one day He will gather the whole world to Himself. But until He does, there are some living in rebellion, not knowing that they belong to Him or that He has redeemed them."[12] There are clearly texts which envisage a universal intent in the atonement (John 4:42; 1 Tim 2:6; 1 John 4:14), where

9. Kaufman, "Religious Diversity," 5.
10. Newbigin, "Religious Pluralism," 50–54.
11. Sanders, *What of the Unevangelized?*, 6.
12. Sanders, *What of the Unevangelized?*, 20.

Jesus is Savior of the world. There are other texts which contemplate a particular purpose in Christ's death (Matt 1:21; John 10:11, 15; Eph 5:25; 1 John 3:5). Whatever position one might take on the intent and extent of the atonement, the point is that Scripture nowhere indicates that all will ultimately be saved, and God's plan cannot be frustrated by man's will. God has provided a sufficient atonement for all which will be efficacious only for those who believe. Kuiper expresses the Reformed position:

> The Reformed theology insists that God Himself, who has determined from eternity who are to be saved and who are not . . . makes on the ground of the universally suitable and sufficient atonement a most sincere, *bona fide*, offer of eternal life, not only to the elect but to all men, urgently invites them to life everlasting, and expresses the ardent desire that every person to whom this offer and this invitation come accept the offer and comply with the invitation.[13]

Whatever tension we might have in reconciling divine sovereignty and human responsibility, God "works all things according to the counsel of his will" (Eph 1:11). He overcomes resistance and rebellion to lead sinners to saving faith in Christ. God's sovereignty is compatible with man's moral accountability. We affirm it even if we struggle to understand it, and we sow gospel seed indiscriminately without knowing the outcome. That God knows is sufficient! The danger lies elsewhere in the denial of the centrality of Christ as the only one who saves apart from good works or religion.

John Hick is one of the towering figures in the current debate on the extent and nature of salvation and he cannot be ignored. Although he points to having begun his Christian life as a fundamentalist and to his evangelical conversion, he has clearly discarded his evangelical roots.[14] While teaching at Princeton Theological Seminary he "questioned whether belief in the Incarnation required one to believe in the literal historicity of the Virgin Birth."[15]

---

13. Kuiper, *For Whom Did Christ Die?*, 86–87.
14. Hick, "Pluralist View," 29–30.
15. Hick, "Pluralist View," 32.

Soon he joined those "thinking Christians" who have increasingly abandoned exclusivism.[16] We will be often reminded that the exclusivist position is one of intolerance and ignorance. Hick states unequivocally that as Paul "wrote about the saving activity of God the inner logic of that which he was writing inevitably unfolded itself into the thought of universal salvation."[17] On Jesus' warning in Matt 25:46, that "these will go away into eternal punishment, but the righteous into eternal life, " he asserts,

> Jesus was neither propounding a theological theory nor defining theological doctrines... Jesus was not discussing the general question whether anyone ever has remained or ever will remain in this state beyond the point of no return [and] his grave warnings . . . do not necessarily conflict with St. Paul's indications, in the more detached theological mode, of a final universal salvation.[18]

Of course, Hick does not believe that Jesus actually spoke these words but that the church in succeeding generations attributed them to him. According to his confident assertion, "We should not think of the four Gospels as if they were eyewitness accounts by reporters on the spot. They were written between forty and seventy years after Jesus' death by people who were not personally present at the events they describe."[19]

The errors of religious pluralism and universalism are not new even if they are more and more pervasive among those who claim to be Christian. For example, Ernst Troeltsch (1865–1923) wrote *The Absoluteness of Christianity and the History of Religions* in 1901. Later in life he abandoned the absoluteness of Christianity and accepted the view that religion is "*une affaire de geographie*" (a matter of geography) and held to the relative absoluteness of Christianity. Raimundo Panikkar considers Christianity "as one religion among many, and Jesus, ultimately, the savior only of Christians."[20] Arnold

16. Hick, *Myth of Christian Uniqueness*, 16.
17. Hick, *Death and Eternal Life*, 248.
18. Hick, *Death and Eternal Life*, 248–49.
19. Hick, "Pluralist View," 35.
20. Panikkar, "Three Kairological Moments," 91.

Toynbee (1889–1975) held that the great world religions needed to find common ground and should seek "to purge Christianity of the exclusive-mindedness and intolerance that follows from a belief in Christianity's uniqueness."[21] For Paul Tillich, "Religion cannot come to an end, and a particular religion will be lasting to the degree in which it negates itself as a religion. Thus Christianity will be a bearer of the religious answer as long as it breaks through its own particularity."[22] Thus, "Toynbee and a multitude of other writers tend to interpret Christianity 'wholly in terms of ideas' rather than God's decisive intervention in history."[23]

For those who hold to the authority of Scripture there can be no surrender to the uniqueness of Jesus Christ in salvation and the necessity of faith in him. We may not always understand how God is at work in the world among those who have little or no contact with the gospel. We know that God is just, gracious, compassionate, and merciful. We know that he has not left himself without witness with his providential care (Mark 5:45; Acts 14:17). Our responsibility cannot be avoided. God has given us the weighty and sacred task to make Christ known and "has associated His Church with Himself in this urgent task."[24] We can be assured that God will do what he has promised. We need to do what he has commanded us. We must continually affirm our conviction that Christ died as a propitiation "for the sins of the whole world" (1 John 2:2). He calls all people everywhere to repent (Acts 17:30), and one day every knee will bow before him as Lord of all (Phil 2:9–11). All creation will not be ultimately united with Christ in salvation, but all will be in subjection to him (1 Cor 15:28). All will not finally be saved, but as much as lies in us, all should have the opportunity to hear. We have no reason to limit the reach of God's grace or doubt that a compassionate God of love and mercy will do what's just (Gen 18:25). In the end "we may safely leave such to His fatherly care."[25]

21. Toynbee, *Christianity Among the Religions*, 95–96.
22. Tillich, *World Religions*, 96–97.
23. Anderson, *Christianity and World Religions*, 18.
24. Sanders, *What of the Unevangelized?*, 79.
25. Pierson, *Crisis of Missions*, 297.

― Chapter 4 ―

Dreams, Visions, Angelic Visitations

ONCE WE HAVE ESTABLISHED the solid biblical support for the teaching that salvation is in Christ alone, we need to wrestle with the hearing of the good news. Romans 10:17 tells us that "faith comes from hearing, and hearing through the word of Christ." What constitutes hearing, and do people need to hear what we might call a gospel proclamation from a human messenger? If so, how much does someone need to know in order to place their faith in Christ for forgiveness of sins and salvation? We know that God has always had only one means of saving people and that those under the Old Covenant were saved by grace through faith. What is different from our experience is the content of the message. Those living before the Christ event did not hear what we have heard or understand what we now know. God communicated in different ways in the past. At times he spoke personally or spoke through visions and dreams. Even in the Old Testament, a period covering thousands of years, God mostly spoke through his prophets (Heb 1:1). Dreams, visions, and angelic visitations were relatively infrequent. They were never the ordinary means for God to communicate with his people. A great deal of research has been done in the area of dreams. J. Dudley Woodbury is well-known for his survey of reasons Muslims came to Christ. Dreams figured prominently in many testimonies.[1] We don't need to accept the validity of these dream stories but it is difficult to completely discount all of them.

---

1. See Woodbury, *From Seed to Fruit*.

While I remain suspicious of any attempts to normalize them, I'm not in a place to completely rule them out.

In any case there is not the expectation that in our day, with the God-given revelation we possess in the sixty-six books of the Bible, that we will hear God's voice or encounter him in our dreams, visions, or receive angelic visitations. God spoke to Old Testament believers through the prophets and has now spoken to us by his Son (Heb 1:1–2). We believe in the sufficiency of Scripture to point and lead people to Christ through whom God has authoritatively spoken. Dreams, visions, and visits by angels are not as common in the New Testament period as some would have us think. There are clusters of these phenomena around the time of Christ's birth (Matt 1:20; 2:12, 13, 19, 22; Luke 1–2) and a few other references to dreams found elsewhere (Matt 27:19; Acts 2:17; Jude 8). I agree with Sinclair Ferguson that "we should probably beware of people who claim that God regularly reveals himself to them through dreams or by angel visits."[2] This holds true for those today who claim God is speaking to them and through them.

One popular "Christian" book series consists of conversations recorded by someone who needed more than the Bible and sits with pen and paper to record what Jesus is saying. Actually, the problem is not that what Jesus purportedly says is wrong. The recorded words are mostly exhortations, admonitions, and good advice. The error is claiming a personal connection with Jesus who is speaking to this person as she records his words. My response, tongue-in-cheek, to those who might claim to have a special message from God to me is simply that I struggle to obey everything I know God has revealed in his word and don't need anything else to struggle with. My theological response is to flee from anyone who claims to hear the voice of God and to record his words outside Scripture.

My theology concerning Scripture has not changed in almost fifty years in the Christian life and Bible study. I believe that the word of God as revealed in the sixty-six books of the Bible is his final, authoritative, inerrant, and infallible written revelation

2. Ferguson, *Redeeming Grace*, 45.

to which nothing can be added. I also remain open to the possibility that God might operate outside my theology and comprehension in unique and rare circumstances which in no way add to or undermine the authority of Scripture.

Several years ago I had a conversation with a Christian of Muslim background. He shared the story of his childhood in a Muslim village in a North African country. There were no Christians, there were no Bibles, there was no testimony to the gospel, and there had been no missionaries. He had a dream in which Jesus spoke to him and told him that he was the Way, the Truth, and the Life. The dream did not lead to an immediate salvation response, but it led him to acquire a New Testament, and he began a journey that eventually led to his conversion and transformation. What would you say to this man? Here's a Christian brother standing in front of you with a sweet and powerful testimony of a changed, gospel-centered life, a brother in Christ who since his conversion received significant theological training, a servant of God now engaged as a leader in Muslim evangelism, and someone who has paid a high price for betraying his ancestral religion and dishonoring his family. Of course, I had several questions for him. I suppose I was probing to better understand something that didn't sit well with me or fit into some of my theological boxes. There remains something of the skeptic in me, and I generally start with a stance of suspicion when anyone makes claims for this type of experience. What I discovered was that the reported dream was a one-time occurrence, an event this man could not rationally explain and something he did not propose as normative for others or necessary in his evangelistic endeavors. What do you make of his dream? You can deny it and say it never happened—which doesn't mean it didn't. You can accuse the man of lying, being delusional, or inventing the story for his own benefit. Or can you thank the Lord that this man who was once lost is now found?

A reading of the book of Acts provides a stark reminder of the distance between the first-century world of the apostles in the early church and our own. The preaching of the gospel was often accompanied by apostolic "signs and wonders and mighty works"

(Acts 2:22, 43; Rom 15:19; 2 Cor 12:12; Heb 2:4). There were instances of healings, speaking in tongues, and even raising people from the dead. The arrival of gospel-bearing messengers was also occasionally preceded by dreams and visions, most notably with Cornelius in Acts 10 and the Macedonian call in Acts 16:6–10. God also intervened miraculously in other ways as in the earthquake in Philippi followed by the conversion of the jailer and his family (Acts 16:25–34). Surely some of these amazing events were programmatic in the progress of the gospel, in movement from the initial Jewish emphasis in order for the gospel to finally break out among the Gentiles in crossing ethnic, cultural, and religious barriers. The gospel went from Jerusalem to Judea, to Samaria, and then to the outermost reaches of the Roman Empire (Acts 1:8). With each new breakthrough there were miraculous accompaniments to the gospel as confirmation, mostly to skeptical Jews, of the inclusive invitation and nature of the good news and the exclusive message of salvation in Christ alone (Acts 4:12).

Keep in mind that Jewish apostles and early Jewish believers experienced considerable difficulty in accepting the inclusion of Gentiles into the new community. God used a vision to enlarge Peter's truncated perspective in order that he might begin to envision the wideness of God's gracious offer of salvation that included those outside the historical redemptive stream. Peter was familiar with the centripetal emphasis of the Old Testament where outsiders were brought into the national entity of Israel as the center of God's redemptive plan. God was now directing a radical centrifugal movement where Jewish believers would move out from their nation and take the good news to Gentiles who would not need to embrace Judaism. Apart from certain proscriptions (Acts 15:28–29), Gentile believers did not need to submit themselves to Jewish practices and cultural scruples.

Many have erred in building whole movements on the expectation of the miraculous as we will see in the next chapter. Yet at certain times, few in number over a period of several decades, there were manifestations of tongues and the descent of the Holy Spirit, which were reminiscent of Pentecost (Acts 2). This is most

DREAMS, VISIONS, ANGELIC VISITATIONS

clearly seen when the gospel arrived to the ethnically-mixed Samaritans (Acts 8), God-fearing Gentiles (Acts 10), and disciples of John the Baptist (Acts 19). Interspersed between these unique events are miracles that convincingly demonstrated the arrival of a new era, the inauguration of the reign of God in an already/not yet fulfillment of Old Testament prophecy. Truly a new age had dawned with evidential signs and wonders to herald the incipient arrival of new covenant realities. Thus, the discontinuity we observe between the age of Acts and the age in which we live may require little explanation. Others are free to disagree, but when I consider the paucity of similar events recorded in church history, I must conclude that dreams, visions, and angelic visitations, although not limited to a few first-century decades, are not normative today. A number of reasons support this assertion.

The apostolic age was clearly one of transition, a time when the New Testament writings were not yet complete, and apostles and prophets were foundational for the church (Eph 2:20). Now that we have the complete word of God, we should no longer expect to see manifestations analogous to what took place in the book of Acts. Support for this view is found in several places. First Corinthians 13:10, "when the perfect comes, the partial will pass away," is a standard prooftext for the cessation of Acts-type phenomena. The word "perfect" is interpreted as "the full or complete revelation that God has decreed for the church—a reference to the New Testament canon."[3] Others however view "the perfect" as the end of this dispensation[4] or "the end of cosmic time."[5] I realize that this text alone is not decisive in resolving the issue at hand and the interpretive challenges of this text, although I lean toward the first view, the cessation of God's revelatory activity for the church. Perhaps a stronger argument for my view is the scarcity and apparent diminution of supernatural activities as the first century ran its course. After all, Jesus performed his first miracle at Cana in transforming water into wine after thirty years of earthly

---

3. Compton, "First Corinthians 13," 38.
4. Grosheide, *1 Corinthians*, 309–10.
5. Kistemaker, *1 Corinthians*, 467.

existence. His miracle activity was concentrated in the three or so years of his public ministry. Paul, at the end of his ministry, speaks about leaving Trophimus ill at Miletus (2 Tim 4:20). Did Paul lose the ability to heal or was it simply God's will for Trophimus to remain sick? We really don't know. In either case, there was no normative expectation for a miracle.

Can we find middle ground between extreme positions—a total refusal to accept any divine intervention through dreams or visions, and aberrations of experience and anecdotal-driven movements? Personally, if I have to categorize my view on the possibility of God's supernatural interventions in the progress of the gospel, I would prefer to characterize myself as a "soft" cessationist—that is, closed to any new revelation for the church but open to the possibility that God may in fact use dreams, visions, and angelic visitations today, with the emphasis on "may." I must admit my reticence for many years to espouse this position. My theology—or better, my "theological environment"—did not allow for what seemed to be credible evidence that God freely chooses at times to reveal himself in Cornelius-like fashion to those who have no access to the gospel. Furthermore, I see no biblical warrant to not remain open to the possibility of God's supernatural intervention if he so decides. As we have seen in the book of Acts, this activity might be limited to unique pioneer situations or where there is no access to the gospel or no Scriptures in the vernacular. This does not lead to seeking visions, dreams, and angelic visits as integral and common occurrences in mission. After all, parsimony was the rule for dreams and visions in that God used them sparingly. Yet neither should the possibility of present-day dreams and visions be categorically and dogmatically denied because we don't experience them, seek them, or need them since we have the final authoritative word of God. I cannot discern with certainty the origin and source of all professed mystical experiences. There might be demonic activity or human delusion, but I lean toward the view that "an enormous proportion of them have their origin in the subconscious mind of the person concerned."[6]

---

6. Anderson, *Christianity and World Religions*, 41.

DREAMS, VISIONS, ANGELIC VISITATIONS

It must be granted that our experience, along with tradition and reason, has a part in shaping or informing our theology. On one hand, experience has led me to a greater openness to what God might be doing in the world today. Not my personal experience, mind you, since I have had no visions or dreams and have no expectation of any. When the experience of others from primarily unreached regions or unique situations does not contradict or violate Scripture, we must proceed cautiously. We should test all claims by Scripture and refuse to naively accept all anecdotal "evidence" for the miraculous. We should consider the source and the reliability of the witnesses. Two examples come to mind. One was a seminary professor teaching in English in a remote area through a translator. There were people who spoke another language for which there was no translation provided. They claimed they heard the teacher in their language without a translator. Another friend ministering in the Far East recounted praying for a man who appeared deathly ill and who was revived before his eyes. These stories are still anecdotes but in my opinion, considering the sources, of high probability.

My concern is that we do not deny that God can do "far more abundantly than all we ask or think" (Eph 3:20). I must admit that there is also the longing that it might be so, that God might be at work among those places and peoples the gospel has not yet reached, in those settings where gospel proclaimers are barred from entry, and where proclamation is prohibited. On the other hand, while experience may lead us to more openness to God using dreams and visions in light of all the accumulated accounts, and there are many, we should not see these experiences as an end in themselves. I do not propose naively and rashly accepting every dream and vision anecdote as genuine. No one can accuse me of promoting infatuation with the spectacular. We often wrestle, however, with the tension between what we see, what we want to see, and what is real. In the authoritative word of God "we have the prophetic word more fully confirmed" (2 Pet 1:19) to which we must give our attention. The possibility of dreams and visions, a very real if rare possibility in my opinion, must not distract us from our task to proclaim Christ and make him known in every place. Yet we must not be fearful that God might work in ways which surprise us and perplex us at times.

The apostle Paul's ambition as a pioneer evangelist was "to preach the gospel, not where Christ has already been named" (Rom 15:20), evangelizing and planting churches where the gospel had not previously been preached. Our pressing ambition should be to reach those regions where Christ is unknown. Until we complete that task, perhaps we might hold in abeyance our refusal to allow God to work in ways we do not personally experience in our gospel-saturated culture. Perhaps we should pray that he would work in supernatural ways in those places where the name of Christ remains unknown. As for me, I rejoice that God is at work, tirelessly accomplishing his purposes. And if he deigns to use dreams and visions in those places where there is no gospel light, then I will bow and praise him.

―――― Chapter 5 ――――

Signs and Wonders in Missions

THE PREVIOUS CHAPTER MIGHT lead to some questions concerning signs and wonders and the extravagant claims made for healings in our day. I want to remove any confusion by asserting that today's Signs and Wonders movement bears no resemblance to the signs and wonders we see on the pages of the New Testament during the early days of the church. An assertion is not proof but I believe that an honest reading of the New Testament points us in that direction when we compare signs and wonders in the first century and the Signs and Wonders movement in our days. I agree with Schnabel who writes, "The assertion that the miracle promotes faith and should thus be an integral part of the mission and evangelism of the church is neither confirmed by Paul, by Luke's narrative of the apostles' missionary work in the book of Acts, or by the history of the church."[1] Miracles often provoked antagonism as in John 11 following Lazarus' restoration to life. John tells us that many of the Jews believed in Christ "but some of them went to the Pharisees and told them what Jesus had done" (vv. 45–46). The Pharisees and chief priests recognized that Jesus was doing "many signs" and devised a plan to rid themselves of him rather than lose their place and their nation (vv. 47–49). As long as the apostles were alive and the word of God was not yet completed, God worked in uncommon and miraculous ways to point people to the Lord Jesus Christ as Savior. I remain open to God working in ways that do not fit

1. Schnabel, *Paul the Missionary*, 454.

into my thinking and don't expect all my readers to agree with my assessment of the place of signs and wonders in missions today. I also remain resolutely opposed to the counterfeit movements of our day and to their practitioners.

You will notice several references in this book to Charles Kraft, a well-known missiologist who has made important contributions to mission studies and has helped me in my own reflection on mission practice, especially in his book *Anthropology for Christian Witness* (1999). Even in that book Kraft had an interpretive agenda and controversial discussions on power encounters. He asserted, "Unfortunately, the majority of Christian witness coming from the West has neglected the advocacy of power encounters in the presentation of the Gospel."[2] He does not neglect or diminish the importance of truth encounters but emphasizes the necessity of power encounters in power-oriented societies. Over time, Kraft's thinking shifted to fully embrace the Signs and Wonders movement popularized by John Wimber. As a result of this shift, Kraft wrote *Christianity with Power* (2005). Since then he has written extensively on power encounters and demon possession, but in this chapter I want to highlight some of Kraft's dangerous teaching from *Christianity with Power*. One cannot read this book without sensing something of the frustration of Kraft's pilgrimage from traditional evangelicalism to an engagement in a healing ministry through power encounters. Signs and wonders form an intricate part of his ministry and need to be examined not only through his eyes but ultimately scrutinized by the light of Scripture. There are many disconcerting elements of great concern to evangelicals who have not undergone the paradigmatic shift experienced by Kraft.

All believers accept the validity of signs and wonders in the past and in the inaugural kingdom ministry of Christ, and many recognize these signs as also belonging to the future instauration of the millennial reign of Christ. It is also accepted as axiomatic that God can and does intervene miraculously in the affairs of men. Research from credible biblical scholars provides support for miraculous healings throughout the world, a miracle described

2. Kraft, *Anthropology*, 452–54.

as "a divine action that transcends the ordinary course of nature and so generates awe."[3] The numbers of testimonies are staggering although "because of different assumptions, different people require different standards of evidence."[4] They may not all be true. It is unlikely that none of them are true. Many people engaged in cross-cultural ministry have seen God work in unexpected, indeed miraculous ways, while normally working supernaturally through the means of the ministry of his word through the power of the Holy Spirit. And Craig Keener observes that "the most dramatic miracles happen most often (though not by any means exclusively) on the cutting edge of evangelizing unevangelized areas, a setting similar to the one in the Gospels and Acts."[5] I don't know that I would describe anything I have experienced as direct, irrefutable, divine, miraculous intervention, but as I wrote in the last chapter I know credible witnesses who have. As John Piper says, "Whether we are involved in power encounters where demons are cast out dramatically, or in the more typical, but just as supernatural, work of deliverance by Spirit-empowered preaching and teaching and counseling, the summons of faith is the same."[6]

Where I would part with Kraft is his insistence on the necessity of power encounters and his developed methodology for healing and deliverance. In *Christianity with Power* Kraft calls on believers to critically analyze their worldview assumptions and understand the detrimental and soul-stifling results of Enlightenment thinking. Kraft wants us to be open to the reality that God works today through power encounters. Of course, believers should remain open to having convictions challenged, modified, or sharpened by the word of God, no matter how deeply and sincerely held. Yet Kraft's lack of clarity, proof texting, and dependence on anecdotes are troubling aspects of his advocacy of the Signs and Wonders movement. The rampant subjectivity does

---

3. Keener, *Miracles Today*, 3.
4. Keener, *Miracles Today*, 1.
5. Keener, "Miracles," para. 23.
6. Piper, *Providence*, 259.

little to remove the cloud of doubt that lingers in the minds of many concerning the validity of this movement.

Kraft challenges the Christian worldview influenced by the Enlightenment (1680–1790), the culprit for much of the distortion in evangelical thinking. The Enlightenment becomes a focal point because of its suspicion of the supernatural and its elevation of reason. His references to the Enlightenment leave no doubt in his mind as to the defective thinking of Westerners bound by a worldview that originates from a system of philosophical skepticism.[7] These observations from a leading missiologist are not easily dismissed; neither are they conclusive, indisputable, or in this writer's opinion worthy of being embraced. I leave it to others to decide for themselves. Certainly in the Enlightenment, as with any movement, most claims can be justified in some place or time.

The Scottish philosopher David Hume (1711–1776) contributed to the skepticism with which miracles are regarded today with his dismissal of the validity of miracle claims. He defined a miracle as "a violation of the laws of nature," as with a dead man who might come back to life, but states emphatically that such a thing "has never been observed, in any age or country"[8] and confidently claims "there is not to be found, in all history, any miracle attested by a sufficient number of men, of such unquestioned goodsense, education, and learning, as to secure us against all delusion in themselves."[9] He then appears to violate his own standard of proof for accepting a miracle when he recounts the evidence for the healing of Blaise Pascal's niece and then denies it in questioning the motives of those who attested its validity.[10] Hume's influence is alive today. Yet I am not convinced that Kraft's critique of the Enlightenment supports his arguments for the suspicion or denial many have toward unverifiable claims of miraculous events. God has never ceased to be the God of miracles and works beyond what we

---

7. Kraft, *Christianity with Power*, 31–32.
8. Hume, *Enquiry*, 83.
9. Hume, *Enquiry*, 84.
10. Hume, *Enquiry*, 129–30.

can ask or think (Eph 3:20). To recognize what God can do neither requires accepting nor denying all claims about what he has done.

Any strengths of Kraft's book are overshadowed by its glaring weaknesses. One of the most significant is the importance of experience which neglects crucial theological considerations and exegesis. The influence of a Signs and Wonders course in 1982 was pivotal for him and what took place in the classroom "reminded [him] of New Testament days."[11] He cannot overestimate the importance of John Wimber to whom Kraft is indebted and admits the part experience had in his paradigm shift.[12] The experience of spiritual power explains the rapid growth of Pentecostalism, a movement formerly viewed with suspicion by Kraft and now embraced. Here he sounds strangely similar to Hume for whom "experience [is] our only guide in reasoning concerning matters of fact."[13]

The prominence of experience is coupled with the necessity of practice until a habit is formed and the need to "try the 'fail fifty times in a row' experiment."[14] Kraft has experimented in five areas of exercising spiritual power. While recognizing that most of his own healings are small—stomach ailments, headaches, chest congestion—he has seen hundreds of relatively small physical healings and lays claim to some more important apparent healings. He claims a 50 percent success ratio and admits that Jesus had 100 percent. He felt at the time of writing that his own specialty was skeletal framework, especially lengthening legs.[15] Lest anyone think that Kraft sought a ministry of power encounters, he assures us that it was against his will. He considered dropping out of the ministry and confesses his "weak ability to imagine [himself] as a healer."[16]

To his credit, Kraft does take care to avoid some of the excesses of the modern healing movement. He advocates showing

11. Kraft, *Christianity with Power*, 122.
12. Kraft, *Christianity with Power*, 96.
13. Hume, *Enquiry*, 79.
14. Kraft, *Christianity with Power*, 98.
15. Kraft, *Christianity with Power*, 126–27.
16. Kraft, *Christianity with Power*, 95.

little emotion and questions the validity of mass meetings and "assembly-line" healing, where few are healed in relation to the number seeking healing.[17] Yet he doesn't succeed in distancing himself from the bizarre, including the Lord bouncing a man on his chair while healing him, and the lady whose ears were healed at different times because the Lord told her that one ear was Kraft's to heal.[18] Kraft does recognize the greatest miracle as the salvation of souls and draws the application that, comparatively speaking, casting out demons is not a big deal.[19] His 1–10 scale for demons appears to be motivated more by the need to explain the unexceptional nature of much which is called demon possession. Many would oppose his view of demon possession or demonization of believers, as related in the case of a Spirit-filled woman with nineteen demons.[20]

This book has the potential to create great confusion. Of course I do not recommend the book or Kraft as reliable guides, but his influence cannot be avoided. Most believers experience the frustration of not knowing the reality and power of God in a greater way. Does Charles Kraft have the answer? His sincerity may be compelling to many, yet the lack of theological grounding for his experience and his reliance on anecdotes leaves one suspect. Of course, he would consider that reaction as normal from a Western, Enlightenment-influenced Evangelical. Certainly, we should be more open to allowing God to work in ways that exceed our expectations and experience. Yet these should not drive us into the subjectivism that has heavily affected Charles Kraft. His yearnings are real and find an echo in our lives. In my mind, however, his arguments are neither persuasive nor theologically satisfactory. The Signs and Wonders movement fails to meet biblical criteria and is unconvincing in its claims and alluring promises. An unflagging commitment to biblical orthodoxy must remain an expectant faith, neither denying what God has done and can

17. Kraft, *Christianity with Power*, 141.
18. Kraft, *Christianity with Power*, 148.
19. Kraft, *Christianity with Power*, 103
20. Kraft, *Christianity with Power*, 128–30.

do, nor uncritically accepting all that has been ascribed to him. Mission practitioners will need to wrestle with these issues. I've come to my own conclusions after years of study and ministry. Others must come to their own.

― Chapter 6 ―

Reflections on the Gospel of the Kingdom

The kingdom of God, in both its present and future aspects, figures prominently in the New Testament. But as N. T. Wright observes, "*kingdom of God* has been a flag of convenience under which all sorts of ships have sailed."[1] These ships are social, political, nationalistic, and theological. In spite of these excesses, multiple texts in the New Testament demonstrate that the preaching of the kingdom was the message of Jesus and the apostles (Luke 4:43; 9:1, 2; 10:1). Jesus "instructed the seventy to proclaim, 'The kingdom of God has come near to you'" (Luke 10:1, 9). He announced, "I must preach the kingdom of God to the other cities also, because for this purpose I have been sent" (Luke 4:43). Before his ascension, Jesus appeared to his disciples "during forty days and speaking about the kingdom of God" (Acts 1:3). In Acts we find Philip "as he preached the things concerning the kingdom of God and the name of Jesus Christ" (8:12). The apostle Paul in Ephesus "went into the synagogue and spoke boldly for three months, reasoning and persuading concerning the things of the kingdom of God" (19:8). For two years, during his first Roman imprisonment, Paul proclaimed "the kingdom of God and teaching about the Lord Jesus Christ with all boldness and without hindrance" (28:31).

---

1. Wright, *Surprised by Hope*, 203.

REFLECTIONS ON THE GOSPEL OF THE KINGDOM

What has stirred my thinking on this subject is a study of the Gospels, in particular the Gospel of Mark, and the announcement of the kingdom. The opening of the gospel clearly announces, "The beginning of the gospel of Jesus Christ, the Son of God" (1:1). Jesus arrives on the scene, "proclaiming the gospel of God and saying, 'The time is fulfilled, and the kingdom of God is at hand; repent and believe in the gospel'" (1:14). The phrase "at hand" can certainly be understood as referring to something still to happen. However, when taken with "is fulfilled" it becomes difficult to imagine that at the time when Mark penned this gospel, or now almost two thousand years later, that "the kingdom is at hand" means that it is yet to come. One cannot read the New Testament without seeing that the kingdom of God was central to the teaching of Jesus (Matt 4:23–24) and the apostle Paul, and its proclamation was "an authoritative summons to obedience—in Paul's case, to what he calls 'the obedience of faith.'"[2]

So was the gospel of the kingdom which Jesus preached the same gospel as that preached by Paul and the same gospel preached by God's people today? Or was the gospel of the kingdom announced by Jesus replaced by the gospel of grace or the "Christian gospel?" Liberal scholars have often tried to set Paul against Jesus although Paul claimed to have received his revelation from Jesus (Gal 1:12), and anyone who preaches a different gospel is accursed (1:9). The early apostles, in giving Paul the right hand of fellowship, recognized he was preaching the gospel they preached, the same gospel Jesus preached (Gal 2:6–9). Certainly after the resurrection there was more content to the gospel (1 Cor 15:3–4), the same gospel but from different vantage points. But the heart of the gospel has always been "the narrative proclamation of King Jesus."[3]

Interpreters often begin with theological pre-commitments and then understand references to the gospel of the kingdom within a pre-established framework. This is true of dispensationalists as well as covenant theologians where adherence to a system

---

2. Wright, "Saint Paul," 46.
3. Wright, "Saint Paul," 45.

virtually predetermines the outcomes. A dispensational premillennialist who holds to a programmatic distinction between Israel and the church most naturally sees the kingdom as almost, if not entirely, future. The kingdom refers to the reestablishment of national Israel in the Promised Land during the millennium. A covenantalist who sees Israel replaced or relocated in the church easily moves to an understanding of a present kingdom with no earthly fulfillment apart from the new heaven and the new earth (Rev 21:1). There are other positions than these and nuances within the positions which cannot be discussed here at length.

The kingdom as found and presented in the New Testament will not permit a facile understanding or be pressed into a one-dimensional box. There are passages which indicate a present kingdom aspect. For example, Jesus told the Pharisees, "the kingdom of God is in the midst of you" (Luke 17:21). Jesus announced, "The Law and the Prophets were until John; since then the good news of the kingdom of God is preached, and everyone forces his way into it" (Luke 16:16). Other passages indicate a future aspect. Jesus speaks of the kingdom as an inheritance: "Come, you who are blessed by my Father, inherit the kingdom prepared for you from the foundation of the world" (Matt 25:34). Some "will see the Son of Man coming in a cloud with power and great glory . . . . When you see these things taking place, you know that the kingdom of God is near" (Luke 21: 27, 31).

The initiation of a present aspect of the kingdom must be distinguished from the consummation of the future kingdom. According to Ladd, "the Kingdom of God involves two great moments: fulfillment within history, and consummation at the end of history."[4] The presence of the kingdom in mystery form must also be distinguished from the church. As believers, God "has transferred us to the kingdom of his beloved Son" (Col 1:13). We are in some sense in the kingdom and representatives of the king and of his reign. As representatives of his reign we seek to extend that kingdom, that reign in the lives of others who become his subjects. There are other stages in kingdom progress both on earth and in the

4. Ladd, *Presence of the Future*, 118.

new creation when we rule and reign with him forever. The reality of future completion does not rule out present realities.

There is a legitimate concern in some quarters that an emphasis on the gospel of the kingdom and its extension leads to prioritizing felt needs, social and humanitarian concerns. In this perspective, while poverty and injustice are matters of concern, since they are not matters of ultimate importance, they are not necessary areas of engagement for the church. A further distinction is often made that Jesus preached the gospel of the kingdom to Israel, and the church preaches the gospel of the death, burial, and resurrection of Christ. In this view, the gospel of the kingdom is connected with the offer and rejection of the kingdom, also known as the postponement theory, a theory which has seen a sharp decline in defenders. It should be noted that those who make a distinction between the gospel of grace for this dispensation and the gospel of the kingdom are clear that in every dispensation salvation has been by grace through faith.

One reason for the renewed interest in this subject is that the gospel of the kingdom speaks of justice, often connected with the phrase "social justice." Biblical justice is a gospel issue. If we received justice from God we would all be lost because we are unrighteous. Christians are justified by faith and made right with God by his grace and mercy. As implications of the gospel we should be concerned about human justice—working with the disenfranchised and seeking justice for the oppressed. Social justice, however, has been enlarged to include issues far removed from biblical concerns. Justice in human hands is often based on human reasoning and a culture of victimhood, and the oppressed are those whose behavior is at times in contradiction to biblical morality. As an aside, I agree with DeYoung and Gilbert in preferring the expression, "loving your neighbors," to the misunderstood and much-maligned phrase "social justice."[5]

We cannot read Scripture without seeing God's concern for the widow, orphan, and downtrodden, a concern we should share. Concern for the poor, the betterment of communities, literacy

5. DeYoung and Gilbert, *Mission of the Church*, 21.

campaigns, community prayer vigils, and the like, while legitimate good works for Christian engagement, must not be confused with the primary mission of the church of evangelism and discipleship. We need to exercise caution here. We are free to engage in good works as legitimate extensions of gospel ministry both as individual Christians and as churches. But there is the danger of being involved in what is called "kingdom work" which prioritizes good works and intentionally or unintentionally minimizes gospel proclamation. Several years ago our church was involved with an annual jazz festival in our community. We set up tables with New Testaments and gospel tracts. We also provided pretzels, water ice, and face painting for children. Many doors for gospel witness were opened. Then one year we were told without a reason that we could no longer offer religious literature. We could've continued with providing pretzels and water ice but decided it was not the best investment of our time, energy, and resources if we could no longer provide gospel literature.

There is the danger of dichotomizing word and deed ministry, ignoring and failing to address the roots and the depth of the ravages of sin witnessed in societal problems. For some churches, the homeless are seen from afar or briefly encountered with sporadic mercy missions forays into the city; poverty is kept at arm's length with occasional endeavors to provide food for feeding the hungry; urban blight is seen on the news but never seen up close since those neighborhoods have been abandoned in the name of upward mobility; gang violence, muggings, and carjackings are something on the news not something around the corner; and high school drop-out rates of 50 percent are unknown in privileged communities. I don't know of anyone ministering in urban areas who does not see social concerns rooted in spiritual problems, problems which the gospel addresses through the message of salvation, bringing transformation, granting eternal life, and offering new life in Christ here and now.

There are no easy answers for the multitude of problems which wreak havoc in many urban areas but there is no lasting change apart from spiritual transformation. As I tell people, there is urban and there is urban. By that I mean that in the same city there are enormous differences in neighborhoods which are often in close proximity. Even in troubled urban areas "two orientations—decent and street—organize the community socially, and the way they coexist and interact has important consequences for its residents, particularly for children growing up in the inner city."[6] I have often been bewildered by suburban churches that invest heavily in "foreign missions," sending children to summer camp in other countries or building churches thousands of miles away, and ignoring people in great spiritual need and poverty who live thirty minutes from them.

In any case, I remain assured and intransigent on the person and work of Christ and have an unwavering commitment to preach Christ and him crucified. The preaching of the gospel for the salvation of souls is of ultimate value because people will live somewhere forever. This truth does not require that we ignore temporary needs. While there is certainly a greater fullness and understanding of the gospel following the death, burial, and resurrection of Jesus Christ, is there any valid reason to understand Jesus' preaching of the gospel of the kingdom as different from the gospel we preach? Is there any reason to deny that there is both a present aspect of the reign of God among his people and an eschatological consummation? Now I realize that there is no plain, objective reading of the text. It becomes difficult, however, to escape the truth that in his coming Christ not only offered the kingdom, although not in the way expected by first-century Jews, he also inaugurated the kingdom and validated his claims as Messiah through miraculous activity. What he offered to Israel was not what they expected. Jesus did not offer a nationalistic, territorial kingdom. That kind of kingdom they would have readily accepted. He offered himself as king and his reign over those who submitted themselves to his authority.

The already/not yet formula used by many theologians is helpful in understanding these concepts. In our personal experience we are already redeemed by the blood of Christ with forgiveness

---

6. Anderson, *Code of the Street*, 33.

of sins yet not yet completely free from sin and temptation. We have an inheritance promised to us in heaven and in the new creation but still live in a sin-troubled world. We are already saved yet complete and final salvation awaits the redemption of the body (Rom 8:23). We already taste of the kingdom among God's people in the church but do not yet experience complete harmony. We have so much already in Christ, but when we look at the world we see crime, violence, child prostitution, human trafficking, drug cartels, dictators, corruption. Christ's kingdom has not yet fully come. So we pray—"Your kingdom come, your will be done, on earth as it is in heaven" (Matt 6:10). Not only do we pray, but we also endeavor by our deeds to oppose evil as it manifests itself in brokenness and in the torn fabric of society.

As Jesus preached the gospel, he also did good (Acts 10:38). Our good works are not a replacement for preaching the gospel but accompaniments to it. We confront homelessness, poverty, injustice, crime-ridden streets, and gang violence with the gospel of God's reign. His reign has arrived in the person of Jesus Christ who in his earthly ministry invaded the territory of Satan and in his death dealt a decisive blow to the forces of evil. As the gospel of God's reign is proclaimed, and as men and women submit themselves to his authority, the already inaugurated, not yet consummated kingdom of Christ is extended. We do not attempt to bring in the kingdom but we bear witness to the kingdom through gospel proclamation. Nothing changes people's lives and to some extent their life situation more than the gospel. Nothing helps the homeless, the addicted, the criminal-minded, religious and moral people, and nothing impacts society more deeply than the gospel. When we preach the gospel of the kingdom as Jesus and the apostles did, we are preaching the gospel of God's grace offered to sinners and God's reign in their lives. Society cannot be redeemed. Sinners can!

― Chapter 7 ―

Poverty Alleviation and the Gospel

SINCE WE ARE CALLED to ministry in word and in deed, and with an emphasis on proclamation and the salvation of souls, how should we view our involvement in society and in ministry to the needs of the body? Bryan Chappell of Covenant Seminary asks the question, "How can a local church make a difference, and how do individual Christians meaningfully reflect Christ's grace, when the disparities of wealth and power in our world are so great?"[1] When our leadership team began to lay the groundwork for church planting in Philadelphia we had to wrestle with this question in a practical way rather than theorizing from the relative safety and comfort of middle-class suburbs and seminary classrooms. Located in a transitional urban neighborhood where urban blight meets white flight we were confronted by the challenges faced as Christians regarding our biblical responsibility to the poor. We are not experts in urban ministry and poverty alleviation. We recognize the complexity of the causes of poverty and confess the failure of many Christians, including ourselves, to address and to engage this issue. We are also convinced that "starting new churches is at the heart of calling people to new life in Christ and forming communities fully devoted to Christ the King and his kingdom."[2]

Some people are born into poverty through no fault of their own and find themselves trapped in an inescapable and infernal

---

1. Corbett and Fikkert, *When Helping Hurts*, 2.
2. Bergquist and Crane, *City Shaped Churches*, 43.

cycle. Others fall into poverty as a result of calamity including natural disasters, unemployment, health problems, or traumatic experiences. In impoverished neighborhoods, "the drug trade is everywhere, and it becomes ever more difficult to separate the drug culture from the experience of poverty."[3] Our response must be rooted in the Bible as we seek to lay a theological foundation for our engagement in dealing with societal problems which in reality are spiritual problems. One cannot read the Bible and remain ignorant of the many passages dealing with the poor, the oppressed, widows and orphans, or remain indifferent to their plight (Jas 1:27). For example, when Paul and Barnabas were given the right hand of fellowship for ministry among the Gentiles, the leaders of the church in Jerusalem asked them to remember the poor. Paul's response was that concern for the poor was "the very thing [he] was eager to do" (Gal 2:10). We should be just as eager to remember the poor. Christianity teaches that all share in the same humanity, are made in the image of God, suffer from the entrance and presence of sin in the world, and are in need of the one and only real solution found in the finished work of Christ.

We are not utopian dreamers with illusions about what we can do to relieve misery in its many forms with our meager resources and limited wisdom. Yet we remain compelled by the gospel to not cast a blind eye toward those in need. We cannot ignore the Old Testament prophetic voices and the New Testament witness that "as we have opportunity, let us do good to everyone, and especially to those who are of the household of faith" (Gal 6:10). Poverty is often about broken relationships which sadly contribute to cycles of violence. Recent research shows that in Philadelphia 50 percent of shootings involved an argument, and "many suspected shooters and victims had previously been arrested or received mental health services from the city. The majority had also witnessed violence."[4] That is not to imply that all poor people are given to violence or that violence is limited to urban areas. Although violence in our country is widespread and touches all classes, yet in

---

3. Anderson, *Code of the Street*, 29.
4. Palmer, "City's Gun Violence Crisis," para. 1.

urban areas there is an "inclination to violence [which] springs from the circumstances of life of the ghetto poor—the lack of jobs that pay a living wage, limited basic public services, . . . the stigma of race, the fallout from rampant drug use and drug trafficking, and the resulting alienation and absence of hope for the future."[5] People are caught in a vicious cycle as "the hopelessness many young inner-city black men and women feel, largely as a result of endemic joblessness and alienation, fuels the violence they engage in."[6] On December 31, 2021 over sixty-five shots were fired on one Philly street wounding six people. The only shock was that no one died in this shooting. The last day of this deadly year began with five hundred and fifty-nine homicides and one thousand, eight hundred and twenty-seven nonfatal shooting victims, the most recorded since the city began tracking in 1960.[7] With this scale of societal problems no easy answers or solutions are forthcoming and most initiatives make little impact.

Even if we have much to offer as a church to our community we also declare that we have much to learn from and about our community and their experiences of life in the city. We do not enter the community with pat answers. We enter to listen and learn from the experience and wisdom of those who live there and from those who serve their communities. We will not see poverty and violence eradicated in this fallen world. We will see lives changed by the gospel. Almost fifty years ago I ran these same Philly streets and was part of the problem—crime, drugs, violence. And I was not born into poverty or a broken home. Imagine the challenges faced by those who grow up in that environment.

It is easy to fall on one side or another of extreme perspectives on the reasons for poverty. Does poverty result from a lack of personal morality and individual responsibility, or from unjust social structures and lack of opportunity? The answer is not either-or. It is both-and. There are those in poverty due to wrong choices, indiscipline, skewed priorities, and wasteful habits. But

5. Anderson, *Code of the Street*, 32.
6. Anderson, *Code of the Street*, 325.
7. Palmer, "Over 65 shots fired," para. 2.

that description fits many who were born with a silver spoon in privileged conditions and yet have abundant resources for which they did not labor and which they squander. There are also those in poverty due to systemic political, economic, and social inequities or ill-conceived social programs which hinder more than help the impoverished. It seems that many government programs exist to keep people minimally cared for in poverty rather than lifting them out of poverty. Whatever the causes for poverty, we may need to re-examine our responses in light of Scripture in order to trouble our consciences and to no longer remain captive to the particulars of history which have led us astray in this domain. In declaring the gospel, we must affirm that it touches and transforms every area of life. It will no longer suffice to neatly divide and compartmentalize the human condition as if the gospel has no power beyond the saving of souls. The power to save souls is the greatest and most important aspect of gospel proclamation. However, word and deed cannot be separated. As Keller says, "mercy and evangelism do not need to be offered at the exact same time, yet they must be coupled, because they are interrelated."[8]

As I mentioned in the last chapter, the appearance of the social gospel in the early twentieth century continues to haunt Bible-believing Christians. They are often unaware that evangelical Christians who lived before the Fundamentalist-Modernist controversies did not hold to the stark dualism that characterizes many Christians and churches today who live in the shadow of the social gospel boogeyman. It is true that there were theological aberrations among those who replaced proclamation of the gospel with deeds of mercy. There were many who did good works under the banner of social justice which replaced the banner of the cross. In reaction to that drift there was a wholesale abandonment of word and deed ministry, an emphasis on verbal proclamation minus deed engagement. In the name of separation from liberals who no longer preached Christ, many Christians avoided being associated with any whiff of social gospel influence, escaped neighborhoods in the throes of change and disruption, and fled to safer communities. Apart from

8. Keller, *Ministries of Mercy*, 113.

occasionally venturing into cities for relief efforts to distribute sandwiches to the homeless or assist at rescue missions, enough to soothe troubled consciences, there has been a tragic absence of long-term engagement with the oppressed and downtrodden. The common retort that "we just preach the gospel" must be seen as an incomplete and truncated understanding of the gospel. Tim Keller, in his assessment of Jonathan Edwards's "Christian Charity" from 2 Cor 8:8–9, argues persuasively "that if you grasp substitutionary atonement in both your head and your heart, you will be profoundly generous to the poor" and that "all sinners saved by grace will look at the poor of this world and feel that in some way they are looking in the mirror."[9] Carson observes that if "we do focus on the gospel and understand it aright, we shall soon see that how this gospel rightly understood directs us how to think about and what to do about a vast array of other kinds of issues."[10]

There is a yearning in our hearts to serve others and to make a difference in the lives of people through planting churches that preach the glorious gospel of salvation and effectively engage and minister to the community. We've experienced God's rich grace toward us and want to confront others with the claims of Christ. At the same time, however, we acknowledge our inability to bring about lasting transformation through human endeavors. Our best efforts may be well-meaning yet misguided. And frankly, some efforts might be a waste of time, energy, and resources. As an example, I recall a Christian radio station organizing clean-ups in city parks, something desperately needed as we saw firsthand at the park just a couple blocks from our house where my wife and I frequently walked. On a designated day earnest and enthusiastic teams of trash collectors parachuted into the city to clean the parks mostly unaided by residents and without much coordination with local groups. Those from outside the community did a great job at cleaning up our park but within a day or two there was no evidence as the park quickly reverted to its previous trash-strewn state with trash on the ground next to trash containers.

9. Keller, "Gospel and the Poor," 10.
10. Carson, "What is the Gospel?," para. 13.

We should care deeply about our communities. We should also think deeply about how to best help them since "social concern without the ministry of word would be a vain offering."[11] Anything divorced from the gospel might meet short-term needs, which is commendable, yet fails to address the deeper and ultimate needs people have. We are confident that the gospel which brings forgiveness and spiritual liberation also provides the power to transform lives and to enable believers to live life as God desires. New life in Christ may not bring about immediate release from poverty. Yet with the restoring of broken relationships, which exist between individuals and God and between individuals and their community, a new direction can be set in motion that impacts every area of life.

We should be wise in how we address poverty, both at home and abroad. Many churches have food and clothing pantries to help the needy in their community. As important as it is to meet these needs, especially in emergency situations, there are often downsides when an unhealthy dependency creeps in or when local merchants lose much-needed business. Our church holds regular outreach events, especially around end-of-the-year holidays, to provide clothing, food, and toys to our neighbors. At Thanksgiving we provide turkeys to needy families. What's the point of doing this? The truth is that there are non-religious organizations that do this on a larger scale and touch many more lives throughout the city. We do it for the simple reason to see God open doors for the gospel and to make Christ known. We are all for meeting temporal needs but are most concerned about spiritual needs. If meeting temporal needs provides the avenue to meeting spiritual needs then we will do what we can with the limited resources we have.

Our church also has ministry in Cameroon. For several years we have been working to train pastors in the city of Yaoundé. Most of the pastors come from remote villages to study with us and return to their villages with tools for teaching and preaching the Bible. During one of our visits we met Cameroonian Christians working with the blind and we began providing white canes for

---

11. Keller, *Ministries of Mercy*, 114.

the blind in Cameroon. We now work with an organization for the blind in Cameroon directed by a blind Christian. Our primary purpose in ministry in Cameroon is not helping blind people. But it is an opportunity that God gave us and has opened many doors for gospel witness. We've been able to attend gatherings during the International Day of the Blind with hundreds in attendance who receive white canes and hear the gospel. These gatherings included dignitaries from other African nations which led to more open doors in other African nations. At the time of writing this chapter one of our elders, a Cameroonian, was working with an organization for the blind to distribute white canes in several African countries. At each step of the way he was able to meet high level government officials and share the good news of the gospel. So we have donated thousands of white canes. Why? As Christians we cannot be indifferent to the physical and material needs of people. It is in our power to help provide a one-time gift that changes the lives of people without creating ongoing dependency on us. Even more importantly, we make it clear in preaching the gospel that God wants to open their spiritual eyes and has promised that one day in his presence they will be made whole.

We are cognizant that not everyone will respond to the gospel and that not all who respond to the gospel will immediately or necessarily experience dramatic changes in their social and economic situation. Moving from poverty to prosperity or from sickness to health are not the primary goals and cannot be promised, although material betterment and wellness may take place. Yet "it is unthinkable that we could truly love an individual and *not* want both to share the gospel as well as to meet the person's basic human needs."[12] The end in view is spiritual transformation in recognition of the lordship of Christ in every area of life and the extension of that lordship, however imperfectly, in our communities and in our areas of influence elsewhere. We look for that eternal city whose "designer and builder is God" (Heb 11:10); we labor and serve here in cities below that by grace we and others might experience a foretaste of what God has prepared for his people.

12. Keller, *Ministries of Mercy*, 110.

―――― Chapter 8 ――――

Israel in God's Program for the Church

Several years ago, Hanna Massad, pastor of Gaza Baptist Church, expressed his dismay at the bombing of his church building during the three-week war between Israel and Hamas.[1] The Palestinian Bible Society also suffered damage from Israeli bombs. In light of these events some questions came to mind. Is present-day national Israel God's people? Do we in this case have God's ancient and now-restored covenant people bombing God's new covenant people, Palestinian Christians in Gaza? Or asked in another way, do we have two peoples of God? Can we be sure that the 1948 United Nations declaration that created modern-day Israel was in fact a fulfillment of biblical prophecy? If so, is there a guarantee that Israel in her present state cannot be destroyed and her people dispersed? At issue is not the right of Israel to exist, which I gladly and unequivocally affirm, but I question the theological justification of a secular state laying claim to God's land promise to Abraham without adhering "to biblical standards of national righteousness."[2]

There are several views on the relationship of Israel and the church. Questions are asked about whether Israel is a type of the church, whether ethnic Israel has a future geographical place in God's plan, or whether the church has replaced Israel as the people of God, as the new Israel. Burge asserts that Paul "thinks of the

1. Weber, "God in Gaza."
2. Burge, *Whose Land?*, 13.

messianic community as having no territorial attachment, but rather having its only attachment to Christ."[3] Further, the lack of Paul's mention of the land "points not merely to the absence of a conscious concern with it, but to his deliberate rejection of it."[4] Romans 9–11 is one of the foundational and controversial passages for the theological significance of ethnic Israel. Few would deny that Israel holds a distinctive place in the history of redemption. And "evangelical Christians have rightly concluded that we of all people have a shared sense of spiritual destiny with Judaism."[5] The differences in views concern mostly the discussion over whether present-day national Israel is the people of God and over God's future work among ethnic Israel. In a recent work on this passage, the contributors "all agree that in Romans 9–11 Israel refers to ethnic Israelites."[6] The debate revolves around how Israel and the church relate in God's redemptive and eschatological plan and whether there will be a future mass conversion of ethnic Jews. For example, Michael Vlach argues that "Paul's understanding of Israel is continuous with the expectation of the OT prophets that Israel is an ethnic and national entity with a role in the world."[7]

An explanation of the views of God's future dealing with ethnic Israel goes beyond the intent of this chapter and are discussed more fully in the book cited above. As with much in the area of eschatology, disagreements will not be resolved until future fulfillment when we all might be a little surprised. I do agree with the observation that "any theological dialogue with and discussion about Israel should distinguish between Israel's place in the covenant of God and the empirical modern state or nation of Israel."[8] There is often an unqualified identification of the modern nation of Israel as the people of God. This viewpoint is often associated with the "two-peoples" view found in traditional

3. Burge, *Whose Land?*, 184.
4. Davies, *Gospel and the Land*, 179.
5. Burge, *Whose Land?*, 10.
6. Compton and Naselli, *Three Views*, 20.
7. Vlach, "Non-Typological," 21–22.
8. Bosch, *Transforming Mission*, 173.

dispensationalism where both ethnic/national Israel and the church are the people of God. This view intensified in the twentieth century with the Holocaust and the founding of the modern state of Israel. Many interpret the United Nations declaration of 1948 through a prophetic lens, which brought national Israel into existence as the fulfillment of Old Testament prophecies. This perspective often requires an almost unquestioning support of a seemingly invincible Israel, rightfully returned to the land and always victorious over its enemies. The myth and aura of Israeli invincibility was burnished over the years by the heroic and courageous spirit of the Israeli people in wars beginning with her independence in 1948. These wars include the Six-Day War in 1967 and the Yom Kippur War in 1973.[9] Although more recent apparent defeats or setbacks have tarnished Israel's image (for example, the July 2006 war with Hezbollah), Israel continues to enjoy popular support in many Evangelical circles as the people of God.[10]

Few Christians would deny Israel's right as a nation to exist, and that "Judaism deserves a place of security—a place to protect itself from outsiders."[11] While some might desire a more proportionate response to the homemade bombs lobbed haphazardly from the Gaza Strip, or oppose the bulldozing of Arab villages in defiance of UN resolutions, no one should question the right of Israel to defend itself.[12] Whether we consider the July 2006 Israeli–Hezbollah War or the more recent Israeli–Hamas War in 2014, what is unquestionable is that more innocent civilians are usually killed and maimed by Israel than by their adversaries. Obviously we can attribute this fact to the sheer supremacy of Israel's American-made-and-supplied armaments. We may also rightfully assert that Israel's opponents often hide among the

---

9. See Herzog, *War of Atonement* for a gripping and inspirational account of this war.

10. See Davis, *Who are the Heirs of the Abrahamic Covenant?* for a fuller discussion of distinctions between dispensational and covenant theology.

11. Burge, *Whose Land?*, 9.

12. Burge, *Whose Land?*, x.

civilian population and fire missiles from apartment buildings and mosques in densely populated urban areas.

Among American evangelicals, 68 percent "believe the Jewish people today have the right to the land of Israel, by virtue of the covenant God made with Abraham."[13] This support is greater among premillennialists than postmillennialists and amillennialists who "do not typically make much of the recent establishment of the state of Israel. Nor do they believe in a thousand-year reign to follow Messiah's appearance."[14] As an American I affirm Israel's right to exist and protect herself from enemies who refuse to recognize her status as a legitimate national entity. I shudder when I think of Israel's history and the diabolical attempts to wipe the nation off the face of the earth. Israel deserves the solidarity of free nations today especially when we recall the long history of European antisemitism and remember that not "a single social group in Europe showed solidarity with the Jews persecuted between 1939 and 1945."[15] Furthermore, I admire a people who live on an island of democracy in a sea of tyranny. I hold them in high esteem for their resolve to resist terrorism and to sacrifice for future generations. Yet as an American evangelical I hesitate to apply Old Testament prophecies concerning the reestablishment of national Israel to the political entity called Israel today.

Theological systems with different hermeneutical assumptions provide diverse responses to the question of the nature and identity of the people of God. New Testament passages which speak of the true children of Abraham as those who have his faith lend support to the "one-people" of God position (John 8: 33, 39–40; Gal 3:7). There are those who argue, however, that the nation of Israel can be identified with the valley of dry bones prophecy in Ezekiel 37. Even if that were the case, it is difficult to conceive of the nation of Israel in its present condition as the people of God. Ultimately, there are theological questions only the word of God can answer

---

13. Casper, "Trump or Netanyahu?," para. 9.
14. Pratt, "Reformed Perspective," 182.
15. Aly, *Europe Against the Jews*, 5.

MISSIOLOGICAL REFLECTIONS ON LIFE AND MISSION

which point, in my thinking, to a unified, redeemed humanity, one people of God composed of Jews and Gentiles.

Dispensational theology sees more discontinuity between Israel and the church than other theological positions and recognizes two peoples of God—Israel, the ancient, original, and prophetic people of God now partially restored; and the church, the second people of God, dispensationally prominent and presently participating in the promises made to the original covenantal people. Ryrie avers "that the Church is not the continuation of Israel and her purpose in being called out from among the nations."[16] He favorably quotes Daniel Fuller's observation that "the basic premise of Dispensationalism is two purposes of God expressed in the formation of two peoples who maintain their distinction throughout eternity."[17] Further developments in dispensationalism have nuanced the idea of two peoples in that "Israel and the church are in one sense a *united people* of God (they participate in the same covenant), while in another sense they remain separate in their identity and so comprise *differing peoples* of God."[18] Dispensationalism is not monolithic, and these quotes are not meant to give the impression that all dispensationalists articulate the two-people view in the same way. Saucy, for example, rejects the "earlier dispensational teaching that divided the people of God into an earthly and heavenly people (i.e., the church and Israel), with fundamentally no continuity in the plan of God on the historical plane."[19] The issue is the relationship of Israel and the church and how that is perceived in relation to the nation of Israel in our day.

Covenant theology, which views the church as the new Israel, may not wrestle with the identification of national Israel, as least not in the same way. Reformed theologians commonly "speak of Israel as the church and the church as Israel."[20] The unity of Israel and the church has been emphasized in Reformed

16. Ryrie, *Dispensationalism Today*, 143.
17. Ryrie, *Dispensationalism Today*, 45.
18. Ware, "New Covenant," 96.
19. Saucy, "Israel and the Church," 239–40.
20. Pratt, "Reformed Perspective," 173.

theology "by applying Old Testament remnant theology to the church."[21] Going further, in speaking of Adam and Eve, Kuiper held that "it may be asserted that they constituted the first Christian church."[22] Hodge maintained that "the Church under the New Dispensation is identical with that under the old."[23] If the church is true Israel, composed of believing Jews and Gentiles, and inherits the promises made in the covenants, then present-day Israel is a nation among other nations—no more, no less. Individuals whose ethnic identity or history connects them with the ancient people of God hold no place of privilege and must enter the true people of God, the new Israel, through the new birth. A Reformed perspective on the unity of God's people, however, leads to the conviction that "Gentiles must carry out evangelism of Jews with a strong sense of indebtedness."[24] These competing theological systems have a long history of debate. They are deeply entrenched as valid viewpoints and hold Scripture in the highest regard, but they differ on interpretive matters regarding temporal and future Israel. The issue of the identity of present-day Israel, however, is less problematic for covenantalists.

Where does this lead us? Is there a way to view present-day Israel in a way that remains faithful to Scripture, does not distort or inflate the place of contemporary national and natural Israel, and does not give the slightest hint of promoting antisemitism? A straightforward reading of the Old Testament lends support to the idea of a future restoration of Israel that has received irrevocable promises (Jer 31:31–37). The question is how those promises will be fulfilled. One's hermeneutic will determine if these promises relate primarily to fulfillment in the future of a national Israel, promises in which the church participates, or if the promises are presently fulfilled in ethnic Israelites, both a

21. Pratt, "Reformed Perspective," 175.
22. Kuiper, *Glorious Body*, 22.
23. Hodge, *Systematic Theology*, 549
24. Pratt, "Reformed Perspective," 176.

present remnant and future "large-scale acceptance of Jesus by Jews before the second coming."[25]

The New Testament reaffirms Old Testament promises that "God has not rejected his people whom he foreknew" (Rom 11:2). The apostle Paul boldly declares "in this way all Israel will be saved" (Rom 11:26). According to Leon Morris, "this expression has caused unending disputation among expositors."[26] Many older commentators took this statement as a reference to "spiritual Israel composed of elect Jews and Gentiles together."[27] Woudstra argues that Jews grafted into "the one olive tree . . . will not form a separate program or a separate entity next to the church,"[28] while Saucy holds that the fulfillment of Old Testament prophecies "is best understood in relation to Israel as a national entity among the nations and not through the church."[29] Reformed amillennialists and postmillenialists differ on the future hope of a mass conversion of ethnic Israel. In spite of their differences, they are united in the conviction that "any large-scale restoration must come through the preaching of the gospel" and "the Reformed vision of Israel's future absolutely dismisses the popular notion that unbelieving Jews will have the opportunity to believe in Messiah when they see him coming in glory."[30]

Covenantal and dispensational scholars have debated texts and interpretation for decades without reaching consensus, and none will be reached in this chapter. I understand the different views on this and the hermeneutical methodologies that lead to different interpretations. I am not overly concerned about how God will accomplish the details of his purposes. I fully expect all our eschatological schemes to be corrected. My struggle is how to relate these texts to the nation Israel in its present state.

25. Pratt, "Reformed Perspective," 184.
26. Morris, *Romans*, 420.
27. Shedd, *Romans*, 348
28. Woudstra, "Israel and the Church," 237.
29. Saucy, "Israel and the Church," 256.
30. Pratt, "Reformed Perspective," 184.

Let's come back to the bombing inflicted on the church building in Gaza. Do we have God's chosen but unregenerate people in Israel bombing God's chosen and regenerate people in Gaza? It seems that much of American evangelicalism and fundamentalism, especially the dispensational varieties, have sometimes married theological views to a conservative political agenda. This agenda not only correctly supports the right of Israel to exist but often excuses her excesses and hesitates to hold Israel accountable for injustices the nation commits. There is the notion that criticizing Israel would make critics enemies of "God's people" and bring them under the curses related to the Abrahamic covenant. Regardless of how we view the place of Israel in prophecy and how we answer the question of Israel's future significance, we might at the very least be more guarded in identifying present-day Israel as the people of God and refrain from mixing our theology and politics into an inflexible theological position. God loves ethnic Israelites and is at work redeeming them worldwide. There are ministries which specifically target ethnic Jews for evangelism and consider the gospel "to the Jew first and also to the Greek" (Rom 1:16) as "a distinctive of the apostle's ministry and message."[31] They need to hear the gospel, and God has called them to repentance and faith in Jesus Christ. Like all peoples, they need to be confronted with the truth claims of the word of God. When they as individuals respond in faith, they will find their place among the people of God.

---

31. Kaiser, "Jewish Evangelism," 40.

Chapter 9

Is Allah the Father of Jesus?

MUSLIM EVANGELISM HAS COME to the forefront of Christian missionary activity for many reasons. Islam, meaning submission to Allah, is the second largest world religion after Christianity, and the fastest growing religion in the world. There were 1.8 billion Muslims in the world in 2015 or about one fourth of the world's population. Most Muslims do not live in the Middle East where Islam originated. The majority live in the Asia-Pacific region with the largest Muslim population found in Indonesia.[1] They "believe that the *Quran* (Koran), the sacred book of Islam, revealed to the Prophet Mohammed in the Arabic language over a twenty-two year period beginning in AD 610, is the timeless word of God."[2] Since the Muslim population in the United States was only about 1.1 percent in 2017, for many Americans their understanding of Muslims and Islam is framed by the tragic events of September 11, 2001. Broadly speaking, today we have two sides in the debate. "One side declares that Islam is inherently peaceful and good—the other that it's inherently violent and evil."[3]

In 2021 our nation commemorated the twentieth anniversary of the world-changing terrorist attack on the United States. Since the 9/11 terrorists were Muslims, in the minds of many, Islam and its followers were lumped together as evil, radical

1. Lipka, "Muslims and Islam," para. 2–4.
2. Gettleman and Schaar, *Middle East Reader*, 12.
3. Kaemingk, *Christian Hospitality*, 2.

IS ALLAH THE FATHER OF JESUS?

unbelievers opposed to faith and freedom. For many missionaries, the last two decades have been a providential season of open doors in the Muslim world and among Muslims who have emigrated to the United States. In any case, we do know God is at work accomplishing his purposes, redeeming people, even his and our enemies, from every tribe, family, and ethnic group. The power of the gospel is on display as multitudes abandon false religion and join the redeemed people of God who one day will gather to celebrate the victory of the Lamb of God and vindicate those who belong to him. Christians, of all people, should want to better understand what is happening in the Muslim world. In this chapter I want to try to clear up one major understanding about the use of the Arabic word "Allah."

During my travels to the Middle East, I heard "Allah" used by Christians in their prayers, singing, and in reading Scripture. It is understandable that to untrained Western ears and in the midst of current world crises that radical Islam comes to mind in hearing the word Allah. At first I myself was somewhat puzzled since in my mind Allah was associated by default with Islam. Since that time, in speaking on the subject of Islam, I have encountered opposition to the idea that Arab believers use or should use the word Allah in referring to God. Most of the objections stem from a misunderstanding of the Arabic language and of the historical and cultural use and development of the word Allah. My short response to objections is that Allah is "simply the word for God, and if you were to talk in Arabic about the God of the Bible, *Allah* is the word you would use."[4] It is unacceptable for American Christians to insist that Arab Christians not use "Allah" and find another word for deity.

How then should we respond to the question, "Is Allah the Father of Jesus?" Whatever the origin of the word, it means "God" or "god" just like the English word. It is true that Allah does not specifically refer to the Christian God. Neither does our English word. Do we require more precision for Arab believers than we do for ourselves? As Christians, of course, we also use Jesus, Jehovah,

---

4. Corduan, *Neighboring Faiths*, 88.

Yahweh, Lord, etc. Arab believers do the same, but in no way does that negate the use of Allah.

Suggesting that Arab believers use the phrase "God of Israel" does little to clarify the issue. Apart from reading "God of Israel" in the Bible, I do not think Arab Christians would regularly or publicly use this fuller name for God, especially in light of the current political situation and armed conflict with Israel. Yet even if someone says, "God of Israel" where "God" translates "Elohim," it would still be "Allah of Israel." It has been objected that since Muslims deny that Allah has a son that Arab Christians cannot proclaim that "Jesus of Nazareth is the son of Allah." I have seen this argument bolstered by the declaration that the "God" of liberals is not the "God" of the Scriptures. Yet, the fact that the God of the liberals is not the God of the Scriptures does not mean we no longer use the word "God." Many religionists use the word "God" to identify someone far removed from a scriptural description. When a Bible-believing Christian says, "I believe in God" and a liberal says, "I believe in God," there is historical and linguistic commonality with theological differentiation. Only deeper investigation reveals what someone means by using the general word God whether in Arabic or in English. It has been noted that in speaking of Allah, Muslims and Christians speak of the same subject but differ in the predicates they say about him. When Arab Christians say that Jesus is the son of Allah, they are saying what no Muslim can say. But they can and do say it because Allah is the normal translation of the Hebrew *Elohim* and the Greek *Theos*.

It is wishful thinking to imagine that Arab Christians should find another word to replace Allah. Certainly, there are words that are needed to fuller qualify the identity of Allah. Perhaps we should frame the issue differently and ask the question, "Is the Father of Jesus the God of Mohammed?" rather than argue about what word to use. Muslims will not call Allah "Father" but Arab Christians do.[5] Additionally, we may be able to distinguish between "God" and "god" in English but for spoken purposes there is no distinction in English and in Arabic there is no capitalization. Or we can

---

5. See Sheikh, *I Dared to Call Him Father*.

IS ALLAH THE FATHER OF JESUS?

ask, "Do Christians and Muslims worship the same God?" To that we respond that "in terms of historical origin, the answer is clearly yes. In terms of theological description, there are many general points of similarity, but when it comes down to specific details, the answer has to be no."[6] Christians worship the triune God—Father, Son, and Holy Spirit. Islam considers Christians "unbelievers because they accept the doctrine of the Trinity."[7] The God of Islam is a "God of power, not a God of love" and is "considered the direct author of *both* good and evil."[8] Theologically, the God of Christians and the God of Muslims is not the same God. We need to clearly articulate "that the distinction between the Bible and the Qur'an or Christianity and Islam is not merely one of competing rituals, but of competing stories that stand behind the rituals."[9]

We should not ignore the fact that historically Arab Christians used "Allah" long before Islam was founded as a religion. Islam borrowed the word which represents two contracted Arabic words "il" and "ilah" (the god). Some have called for Arab Christians to clarify what is confusing for mono-linguistic English speakers who know of Allah only from a biased Western contexts. Why? It is not confusing for Arabic believers. When they say "Allah" they know who they are referencing. Obviously in witnessing to Muslims in an English-speaking context one might prefer using "God" to "Allah." Regardless of what word might be utilized, the identity of God or Allah as the Father of Isa must be made clear and that presents a major stumbling block for followers of Islam. What we must not do is attempt to impose on Arab Christians a burden that we ourselves have not borne, to ask them to deny their history, their language, and their culture in order to appease the troubled minds of American Christians who recoil at the sound of "Allah." If Arab Christians declare "Allahu Akbar," we will respond in kind —"God is great!" In answer to our title question we should respond in the affirmative. For Arab-language Christians, Allah is most certainly

---

6. Corduan, *Neighboring Faiths*, 88.
7. Ankerberg, et al., *Facts on Islam*, 24.
8. Ankerberg, et al., *Facts on Islam*, 24–25.
9. Bennett, *Narratives in Conflict*, 146.

the Father of Jesus who we pray Muslims come to know as the one and true God. We maintain the conviction "that God has designed humanity to be in relationship with him, that only in communion with God can humanity fully flourish and find its true home."[10] For Muslims, who use the same name for God without knowing the reality behind the name, we call them to embrace the lordship of Jesus Christ, the eternal Son of God.

---

10. Kaemingk, *Christian Hospitality*, 19.

──── Chapter 10 ────

Music, Worship, and Missions

Several years ago when I was mission director of a church, one of our missionaries contacted me to discuss an issue he was having with his mission agency. The missionary in question was enjoying fellowship with a pastor at another church. The sister church used different musical styles than the church the missionary was planting. The missionary did not consider the style of music a separation issue. He was serving in a country where there were few sound churches and he longed for fellowship with other believers. The missionary's mission agency contacted him and told him he needed to break fellowship with the other pastor and church because of their compromise on music. The missionary contacted me, anguishing over the directive from his mission agency. I told him that as mission director of his sending church I did not have a problem with his decision to seek wider fellowship and offered to call the regional director of his mission. The director and I had a frank phone conversation. I told him that we, as his sending church, had final authority over the missionary and did not see any biblical reason why the missionary should separate from another pastor and a Bible-believing church because of different music choices. The director told me that the mission agency had certain standards and that leadership had determined that the missionary was in violation of the standards. I knew the director of the mission and some of the men in positions of leadership. None of them had cross-cultural ministry experience. Most of them had pastored

American churches before becoming mission executives. They sought to impose on this missionary their music standards. The basis for their standards was cultural, or part of their sub-culture, and had no biblical support. I told the director that their mission agency was seeking to usurp the authority of the local church. Suffice to say, the missionary soon after left that agency and it is one that I would not recommend to others.

After significant time spent in other cultures I have come to understand that some aspects of worship necessarily reflect our culture, whether in the broad sense of the impact of Western civilization or in regional specificities. In the area of music this can be seen in the effect of classical music influences in many of our majestic hymns, the influence of marching bands in invigorating and outdated gospel songs, and the influence of popular music in many contemporary choruses. We should not expect worship music in other cultures to reflect our situation nor seek to impose our worship language on others. The accoutrements of worship in other cultures may differ. The genre may even offend our sensitivities, but the act of worship and the One worshipped remain the same. We should not be either uncritically accepting of all that is called worship nor rashly refuse to accept the reality that much of which is unknown to us in our worship experience is a worthy and an acceptable sacrifice to God.

I've spent some time in Africa where you can visit African churches and find worship services essentially the same as those in nineteenth-century England, where missionaries were sent forth along with church organs. While the organ may be suitable for worship services in any culture, we should question the wisdom of imposing foreign worship forms on another people. I've also been in Eastern European countries where a piano was not used in church services because of its association with worldly, non-religious venues. While neither the piano nor organ are innately evil and both can be used in the service of worship, they may not always be culturally appropriate in all places. I've worshipped in African churches where swaying and dancing are prominent in their worship and I have joined in within my rhythmic limitations.

Our church does not worship in the same manner although some of our African members sway more than others. There were some African churches, however, which had incorporated elements and movements of dance from tribal cultures which even other African churches cannot embrace. We recognize that our worship forms are but one way in which God may be worshipped. In entering another culture we will be observant and allow believers the liberty to worship God in their own worship language. The "strangeness" of their worship does not necessarily mean it is "strange" worship.

What has been said about other cultures has some application in the diverse cultures of North America. There are great regional and generational diversities that should not be overlooked. There is a music language that we learn and all types of music will not affect all believers in the same way. There are gospel songs my parents loved to sing which hold no spiritual interest or edification for me. I realize, however, that Christians, including my godly parents now with the Lord, are nurtured in a Christian environment where these gospel songs are a staple of their worship. When I hear these songs, I sing them and do not look down on those who hold them dear. I would love to sing these songs again with my parents. Yet we should not expect everyone to sing everything with the same enthusiasm.

My own pre-conversion musical tastes were rooted heavily in the late 60s, early 70s rock culture—Rolling Stones, Led Zeppelin, Grand Funk Railroad—yeah, some of you remember! No, I didn't go to Woodstock but claimed to have been there like thousands of others who wished to vicariously live the legend. After my first year of university studies I had the opportunity to travel as a summer evangelist with a Christian organization. I was a relatively new Christian with two years in the faith. During meetings in a Baptist church in Texas, I was exposed to music that I associated with my past—drums and electric guitars. I was shocked and critical of this worldly-sounding music that was paraded as Christian music. There was no blessing there for me that day as a relatively new convert. I had been grounded in a subculture of Christianity and taught principles of good and godly music. I truly learned to appreciate music that had not been part of my repertoire, a word I use loosely. To this day I enjoy classical music and stately hymns and with others decry the shallowness of much contemporary music. Although I learned a great deal about music at that time, I realized with the passing of time that the authority for many pronouncements made to distinguish between God-honoring and worldly music were not rooted in the word of God. For a number of years I took sides in the worship wars and loudly repeated what I had heard from musical experts who were able to determine what music was acceptable to God. I had lists of good and bad music and sought to dictate musical choices to others. I cannot wholeheartedly embrace everything being written today, or yesteryear for that matter, and still have my opinions and preferences. Although I am convinced that Scripture provides principles to help with our musical choices (1 Cor 10:31; Col 3:16), I am less assured of my ability to determine for others and to call into question all music that sounds strange, worldly, or inappropriate to my ears and tastes. In addition, although there are certainly some exceptions I cannot anticipate, I do not make musical choices a test of Christian fellowship or see these choices as evidence of true spirituality.

 I am not saying that all music is good, that all music is acceptable to God, and that we should shirk our responsibility to declare the whole counsel of God where it touches on this issue. Also, I am not a fan of the church worship model where a worship band performs front and center before a mostly passive and entertained audience. I've known churches that crank up the sound so visitors won't feel uncomfortable. Personally, I want to be part of a congregation that sings and believe Christians can be encouraged and trained in basic practices of congregational singing. I'm simply saying that I am not in the place to make decisions for others to the point where I criticize their choices, call into question their spiritual integrity, or claim to know whether God accepts their worship. He may not accept it and certainly does not accept all that is offered to him as worship. There may be times when there is evidence of that in the lyrics sung and the fruit produced in lives of the worshippers. Yet I do not for a moment think that any group of musical professionals has been charged with the task of authoritatively establishing the guidelines outside of which there is not true worship.

Practically speaking musical choices have to be made. Churches determine what music is appropriate for their worship services and cannot cater to the tastes of every member. And every member should not expect the church music to reflect personal tastes. But after all, who decides? Is it a music pastor or worship leader who decides based on his tastes, preferences, training, and convictions about what constitutes good music? Is it the senior pastor, who may not have musical training but has strong opinions? Each church must decide the procedure for that although I am reticent to have one lone musical guru make these choices and impose his or her musical choices on the entire body.

I'm not suggesting one path to follow or congregational confusion. Some churches have a music team that meets and works in connection with the elders(s) and under his/their leadership. Some churches may allow youth and young adults to use music that might be unacceptable to the entire body in a morning service. For many it's a bitter pill to swallow if they have the impression that the young people are rockin' and rollin' in the youth room. Some might seek a blending of the old and new and, in my opinion, no generation should neglect or lose touch with the great hymns of the faith that accurately teach God's people about him. We should all agree that corporate worship matters enormously to Christians and to God.

During the COVID-19 pandemic with livestream and Zoom gatherings, churches "discovered that being in the same physical space at the same time each week mattered profoundly."[1] As good as it is to have some contact with other believers, we find that digital gatherings offer far less in blessings, edification, and fellowship than we need. Many Christians will continue to gravitate to churches where the music better suits their tastes. Hopefully that will not be their only criterion for choosing where to worship and they will not mistake entertainment for worship.

1. Ross, *Evangelical Worship*, 2.

We may disagree about musical choices but we might consider the reality that God receives worship from music of which we do not approve, and agree that "true worshippers will worship the Father in spirit and in truth" (John 4:24).

— Chapter 11 —

Agreeing to Walk and Minister Together

In our last chapter I talked about a situation where separation was demanded by a mission agency of a missionary who had enjoyed fellowship with a church with different musical choices. Not every issue, difference of opinion, or interpretation is a separation issue. There are times in the Christian life, however, and in the life of the church where we must separate from a believer, church, or Christian organization. The Bible teaches separation; the Bible does not endorse all our practices and understandings of separation. Not everything called biblical separation is really founded on Scripture. I have modified my position on separation over the years and believe it was done in light of a better understanding of God's word. I really believe God changed my position but don't want to blame him for any of my imbalances or inconsistencies. I have been wrong about some things in the past, am wrong today even if I do not see it, and will be wrong on some things in the future.

Ecclesiastical separation from apostasy and from disobedient believers has been one of the hallmarks of some sectors of Christianity. To further define or clarify their understanding of separation, many Christians adopt other descriptive labels as badges of their declared faithfulness to Scripture such as "militant" or "separatist." At times this leads to one-upmanship with determination to be a separatist among the separatists with some standing alone with Elijah because they alone are faithful. We find institutions of higher learning and prominent churches laying claim to the mantle of historic separatism. This often contributes to further division and groundless separation from brothers in Christ. The antics and reactions of many separatists to any appearance of compromise also makes unbiblical separation unpalatable to scripturally-informed and theologically-trained believers who refuse isolationism in the name of separation.

As a biblical concern, separation must be comprehended and expounded although we may too quickly attach "biblical" to our understanding of separation. As an in-house term I readily understand why some would want to be called "separatist" or "militant." Yet I fail to appreciate the emphasis given to such unwieldy and linguistically-charged terms. I further confess that if I were to describe myself or want to be described by others, "separatist" would not be near the top of the adjectival list. Now I do believe in and seek to practice biblical separation although I might be too separated for some and not nearly separated enough for many. Alas, such is the nature of separation when it goes beyond Scripture.

Anyone familiar with the defense of biblical separation has heard the prophet Amos invoked to support the requirement of agreement in order to walk together. Perhaps the phrasing of the King James Version is best known: "Can two walk together, except they be agreed?" (Amos 3:3). Who can argue with that limpid question and the interpretation that agreement is required to walk with other believers? I do not know if I have ever heard an exposition of this verse in its context. What I have heard is a call for separation from other believers in Christ based on a lack of agreement in some area not even remotely connected with the prophet's concerns. Of course, biblical separation does not stand or fall on the misunderstanding of one text. There is abundant New Testament support for separation from unbelief (2 Cor 6:14) and from divisive and disobedient Christians (Rom 16:17; 2 Thess 3:6, 14). Amos 3:3, however, has been hijacked to reinforce an idea of separation which cannot be supported by the text of Scripture. The argument often runs along these lines: "You and I disagree and therefore we cannot walk together. We might agree on a host of biblical questions, especially the fundamentals of the faith, but we disagree on music styles, Bible versions, standards of modesty, church polity, the best Christian colleges and universities to recommend, which conferences to attend, and the application of degrees of separation." *A priori* to this line of reasoning is that in essence one of the two has reached the right position and agreement is required in order to walk together (i.e., fellowship). In that light, Amos 3:3 raises a number of questions about the interpretive integrity of its use to support questionable applications of presumed biblical separation.

The first question deals with the context. Amos 3:3, like all Scripture, was given for our profit (1 Cor 10:11; 2 Tim 3:17). However, the use of this eighth-century BC text as a valid support for twenty-first century biblical separation should be viewed with suspicion when the context is ignored and our present situation far removed from the author's original intent. Amos addresses the people of God and primarily the Northern Kingdom of Israel in verse one with a call: "Hear this word that the Lord has spoken against you." Verse two demonstrates that God had chosen Israel for his special purposes and that Israel was deserving of judgment due to her departure from the living God. The seven questions found in verses 3–8 set forth a cause and effect relationship which evidences the divine right of God to judge his people.

The second question deals with the translation. The King James Version, as noted above, appears to lend itself to the application that there can be no walking together without agreement. Divorced from its context and read from a separatist perspective one can easily understand how the verse might be applied in this way. However, we should consider other translations. The ESV translates this verse—"Do two walk together, unless they have agreed to meet?" Here the emphasis shifts from pre-walk agreement in order to walk together (KJV) to agreement to meet in order to walk together.

The third question deals with the meaning of the Hebrew word "agree." The root word means "to appoint." In its Niphal form it "may also designate making an appointment."[1] Keil and Delitzsch notes the following definition: "to betake one's self to a place, to meet together at an appointed place or an appointed time; not merely to agree together."[2] When we force our twenty-first century definition of "agreement" into the text, we do a disservice to the inspired word.

The fourth and final question deals with the validity of using Amos 3:3 to support current notions of biblical separation in light of the aforementioned. One might ask, "Who are the 'two' in question?" Does this refer to Yahweh and Israel, to an individual Israelite and idols, to Israel and false gods, to the prophets and the Spirit who inspires them, to God and Amos or to God and man generally? Whatever the correct identification may be, which I'll leave for the exegetes, the emphasis is not on being in agreement in order to walk together, but meeting or agreeing to meet in order to walk together. If someone already has their mind made up on "agreement" separation, then Amos 3:3 fits nicely, but the verse does not support biblical separation as preached by many.

If Amos supports anything remotely connected to present-day relationships, it would be the necessity of agreeing to meet with a brother in order to walk with him or at least meet with the brother to determine if walking together will be possible after the meeting. We do not have to agree on everything in order to walk together. Also the level of agreement might differ according to the purpose in walking together. For personal fellowship I can sit down with most any believer in Jesus Christ for a cup of coffee and enjoy hearing of God's work in their lives. When I worked as a hospital chaplain many of the chaplains were women pastors. As a complementarian I do not believe that women should be pastors or elders. That conviction did not prevent us from working together with mutual respect. When I think of church planting, however, there needs to be greater agreement with a co-worker in doctrine and practice than with someone who invites me to speak at their church or conference. I love, appreciate, and respect my paedobaptist brothers

1. Harris et al., *Theological Wordbook*, 388.
2. Keil and Delitzsch, *Old Testament*, 260.

in Christ. I and our church hold to credobaptism and baptize only those who make a credible profession of faith. Paedobaptists believe that the children of believers should be baptized and become members of the visible church. I would accept the invitation to speak at a church or conference with those who practice paedobaptism but would not plant a church with them. I'm not convinced from Scripture of this position and consider it defective. Make sense? Of course, I'm talking about paedobaptists who practice paedobaptism as a sacrament but do not hold to baptismal regeneration as in the Roman Catholic Church.

When working in cross-cultural situations, other parameters for cooperation might be set. About twenty years ago I had the opportunity to travel to a restricted Asian country to investigate opportunities for pastoral training with underground churches. It was difficult working through a translator and trying to understand the doctrine of the believers we met with. So we simplified and narrowed our agreement to what I called then "significant compatibility." By that I meant that they held a high view of Scripture and to the fundamentals of the faith—the Trinity, the deity, sacrificial death, and bodily resurrection of Christ, belief in his second coming, salvation by grace through faith alone. We were able to work together on that basis and as time went on explore areas of divergence. A successful pastoral training ministry continues there to this day.

As Christians we will agree on much and certainly on the authority of Scripture to take us further in our understanding of God's truth. We need to be in agreement with God or moving in that direction without imagining that we have arrived at a point where we can demand agreement from others with us. We may not agree on some things which are peripheral to maintaining and manifesting the biblical unity which exists in Christ. We may disagree in areas of application of biblical principles. We may choose to invite or not invite a brother to speak in our church, to accept or not accept an invitation to speak elsewhere, to collaborate or not to collaborate based on other considerations outside the purview of this essay. Yet we must understand that a disagreeing brother should not automatically be equated with a disobedient brother. It is far too facile to label disagreement as disobedience. A brother's disagreement may be real but it may be with you or me and not with God and his word. And if someone thinks that anyone who disagrees with them disagrees with God, then clearly ignorance is exceeded only by arrogance.

Can we agree to disagree and yet agree to walk together in some measure in the work of God and in the enjoyment of Christian fellowship or at least rejoice at what God is doing in the lives and ministries of others without becoming their critics? One true measure of our understanding of biblical separation may not be how quickly and how often and from how many we will separate, but with how many we will agree to walk together in true obedience and genuine fellowship in spite of our disagreements. Demand agreement and you will find yourself exceedingly lonely and defensive. Seek obedience and fellowship in biblical unity and your circle of faithful co-laborers in the gospel will increase.

— Chapter 12 —

The Gospel and Multi-Ethnicity

FOR THOSE ALIVE IN 1989, who can forget the images of the fall of the Berlin Wall in November of that year? It was one of those defining moments in life where many remember where they were and what they were doing. My family and I were living in France at that time as the television broadcast images of people scrambling over the wall. Throngs of people stood on the wall singing while others with sledgehammers chipped away at that stark, ugly edifice which had separated the German people for decades. We recall President Reagan's earlier words to Soviet leader Mikhail Gorbachev—"Mr. Gorbachev, tear down this wall." A country that had been torn for decades was soon reunited. Anecdotally, several years later I personally met and shook hands with Gorbachev at a dinner where he spoke of his political journey. I was able to address him with "Praise God," a few of the Russian words I knew, to which he responded in kind. The tearing down of the Berlin Wall is only a pale and imperfect analogy to what Christ accomplished at the cross by his death. Through his blood, he brought peace to former enemies, Jews and Gentiles. He removed what the apostle Paul calls in Ephesians 2 the "dividing wall of hostility" (2:14) by "killing the hostility" (2:16) which existed. Christ inaugurated a new state of being and a new state of living which becomes a model for believers today in our quest to experience and to express the reality of being part of the new people of God.

Our church in Philadelphia is committed to "multi-" in many ways—multi-generational, multi-socioeconomic, and multi-ethnic ministry. With a multi-ethnic missional objective we want to be intentional in healing divisions and in celebrating God-given diversity. Our desire has been that Grace Church reflect the diversity of our urban community and the diversity which exists in the body of Christ, not because it's a great idea, although it is; not because we have overcome bigotry and eradicated all traces of prejudice from our hearts, because we haven't; not because it will be easy, because it won't; but because there is a biblical basis for this commitment. Multi-ethnic diversity is God's idea.

When we come to Scripture we need to ask ourselves how the gospel challenges our prejudices and tendencies to tribalism, finding safety in being with people or in a church where most people are much like ourselves. For those who believe the gospel, who are committed to the good news of salvation in Jesus Christ and to the power of the Holy Spirit to effect transformation, there is an answer, and it lies in the world-changing, history-altering events of the incarnation, life, death, burial, resurrection, ascension, and present reign of Jesus Christ. To be clear, I am not criticizing mono-ethnic churches which are such because of demographics. I am critical of a mood, an attitude, which fears or refuses to cross ethnic boundaries and seeks safety among sameness.

There is a fairly recent academic field called hate studies. Whatever the merits of hate studies as an academic discipline, we know why there is hatred—the depravity of the human heart and rebellion against the Creator. Hatred of others expressed in racism is a form of idolatry. It elevates the distinctions of the physical image over the common origin of the spiritual image endowed by the Creator. According to one article in the *Journal of Hate Studies*, we are told that "prejudice and discrimination have an evolutionary basis, rooted in the nature of primate and human subsistence groups." The author asserts "that if prejudice and discrimination can be reduced, then reduction of hatred will follow."[1] The author proposes new techniques or education or

---

1. Fishbein, "Prejudice and Hatred," 113–19.

other limited ways of reducing prejudice and discrimination. He fails to understand that there is no real solution apart from the one God offered in Christ who bore all the sins of the world and has the power to transform the human heart.

We live in a world rife with strife and divisions, hatred of other peoples, where groups of people seek to eliminate other groups because they are different—different religion, skin color, language, and different customs and traditions. We needn't hide or smooth over the reality that the history of our nation witnesses to the wrongdoing against other people including slavery and the forcible acquisition of Native American lands. Slavery was an abomination and blight upon the character of our nation, and sadly, practiced by many who gathered for worship each week in Christian churches to praise God. Many professing Christians lived unchristianly. No one better articulated this hypocrisy and contradiction than Frederick Douglass who with other abolitionists of his day considered slavery "a national sin with many complicitous institutions, none more so than churches and the clergy."[2] Even our Supreme Court was complicit in this evil practice and pronounced iniquitous decisions. We need only look to *Dred Scott v. Sanford* in 1854 which declared that Scott was not a citizen because of his race and slaves were considered private property.[3] After the end of slavery and during the hard years of Reconstruction, "African American church leaders faced the hard work of decontextualizing the culturally captive elements of Christianity into their raw form and then properly recontextualizing them for Blacks in this country."[4] We as Christians should be mindful of the challenges, discrimination, and prejudice minorities experience in our nation today. We are called to model genuine love for all people, to express in visible ways our indifference to ethnic differences. We are not blind to differences, but differences must not divide us. We do not lose distinctions that are still part of our earthly reality. Yet what we have in Christ transcends those differences and those distinctions.

2. Blight, *Frederick Douglass*, 126.
3. Blight, *Frederick Douglass*, 277.
4. Mason, *Urban Apologetics*, 6.

The gospel teaches us that being part of the family of God brings all people to level ground at the foot of the cross. There is no ethnic or racial superiority, no superior culture, and there should be no dominance of one group over another. What counts is that we are "in Christ." Sadly, churches rarely reflect this new covenant reality. In a 1963 speech at Western Michigan University, Martin Luther King lamented that in America the church was still the most segregated major institution in America and 11:00 on Sunday her most segregated hour. Almost sixty years later we need to ask ourselves if much has changed. Actually, research shows that little has changed with 80 percent of congregations composed predominantly of one racial group, and two-thirds of church attendees "say their church has done enough to become racially diverse."[5] We need to ask if we are willing to be agents of reconciliation and open our doors to all people or choose our comfort and traditions over conformity to a colorblind gospel. Many identity categories today are sociological constructs. From God's perspective there is only one race, the human race, although there are many differences relating to ethnicity. Yet we are all descendants of Adam and have a common lineage. Among this one race there are believers and unbelievers.

In Eph 2:11 Paul tells the believers at Ephesus to "remember" what they were apart from Christ. There are some things we need to forget or try to forget but we should never forget what we were before God saved us. In Christ we now have a new identity, a new family, and a new destiny. There are several contrasts in verses 11–22 between our previous condition outside of Christ and our present privileged position in Christ. Our position has changed from outsiders to insiders in Christ (v. 13). Our relationship has changed from hostility to peace since Christ is our peace (v. 14) and came and preached peace (v. 17). Our status has changed from alien to citizen (v. 19). From believing Jews and believing Gentiles God has made both one (v. 14), created one new man (v. 15), reconciled both in one body (v. 16), and granted access to both in one Spirit (v. 18).

5. Smietana, "Sunday Morning," para. 1.

THE GOSPEL AND MULTI-ETHNICITY

In this passage Paul calls on believers to remember the hopelessness of their former condition apart from Christ. They were without Christ, aliens, strangers to covenant promises, without hope, and without God (v. 12). They were far from God and there was a dividing wall which needed to be removed, most likely a reference to the Law. What Christ accomplished at Calvary in removing the dividing wall between Jew and Gentile and in abolishing the "law of commandments" and bringing different ethnic peoples into one body, the church, provides the foundation on which we build in seeking relentlessly to experience and express that unity today.

The division experienced between Jews and Gentiles was an expression of alienation from God. The healing of the division took place at the cross and takes place there today. What a glorious accomplishment! Jews and Gentiles, those who were near and those who were far away, have been brought near by the blood of the cross and peace has been secured. All human efforts, however well-meaning they may be, however wise they may appear from a human viewpoint, are powerless to bring about real change. Laws may be passed that condemn hatred and punish criminal acts against others, but laws cannot change the human heart where the hatred resides.

God is giving his church in our day the opportunity to rectify the wrongs of the past, a past tainted with racism, segregation, and discrimination. Urban churches in particular have the privilege to engage in multi-ethnic ministry that may not be available in mono-ethnic areas. We cannot build multi-ethnic churches since Christ builds the church (Matt 16:18). We cannot coerce diverse ethnicities to worship together. We can, however, be intentional and welcoming in reaching all people with the gospel without regard to their ethnic group or socioeconomic situation.

This poem I wrote several years ago summarizes the message of these verses—from hopelessness and despair to redemption and reconciliation. This is what we earnestly desire to reflect in our community.

It's dark, it's bleak, all is lost, despair;

Division, hatred, racial strife, beware;

All human efforts, worldly wisdom, lead nowhere;

Ah, the Son of God, in human form, our only hope appears;

His sacrifice, His precious blood, our awful sin did bear;

The cross of Christ, His blood made peace, oh hopeless one draw near.

Now reconciled, one body we, what wondrous grace we share.

―――― Chapter 13 ――――

Monocultural Myopia

MONOCULTURAL MYOPIA MIGHT BE defined as defective vision regarding other peoples because of cultural distance. It is a normal condition among those who have had little contact with other cultures and see reality through the narrow lens of their experience. It is not endemic to North Americans but can be found in every society. Yet North Americans may be more severely afflicted because of their geographical and linguistic isolation and notions of cultural superiority. This can be seen in an area as seemingly banal as mapmaking. A study of maps reveals their Eurocentric or Americentric tendency. Looking at maps one might be led to believe that North America (9,385,000 square miles) and Europe (3,800,000 square miles) are larger than the African Continent (11,596,000 square miles). Certainly the difficulties of unraveling a globe to make a flat map might account for some of this lack of proportion. Yet one wonders if other factors might also be at work.

Monocultural myopia should be of particular concern to Bible-believing, missionary-minded Christians because of the powerful and pervasive influence of Western culture and because of the propensity to dress the gospel in Western garb. Non-Westerners in general have long been judged according to their proximity to Western civilization. Savages, pagans, natives, and heathens were those who had not benefited from the marvels of Western technology. The "noble savage" living in relative, idyllic innocence was seen through Western eyes as being blissfully backward. This has been coupled with the expectation that believers and churches in other cultural contexts will essentially mirror Western Christianity not only in its theological presuppositions, as if the last word has been pronounced, but also in its outward expressions.

We all operate out of a worldview, a set of assumptions which we hold consciously or unconsciously about the makeup of our world and the nature of reality. Our worldview becomes the way we interpret our reality and that of others. A monocultural worldview leads to an attitude of superiority which becomes critical of valid cultural differences and various levels of technological competence. Notice that this may be unconscious. Most people do not purposely denigrate those they consider inferior. An attitude of superiority might even lead to the desire for the betterment of others and be viewed as philanthropic. Or the gospel may be presented in such a way as to make it foreign and unappealing to the listeners. As the late missiologist Hiebert perspicuously observed:

> Past missionaries often understood the Scriptures well, but not the people they served. Consequently, their message was often not understood by the people; the churches they planted were often alien, and as a result, remained dependent on outside support for their existence. Missionaries brought with them, not only the gospel, but also Western cultures, and often they failed to differentiate between the two. Many rejected Christ because they rejected the foreignness of the missionary message—not because of the offense of the gospel.[1]

Monocultural myopia easily degenerates into ethnocentrism which judges the actions and attitudes of others through the eyes of someone with experience in one culture with its limitations and biases. Strange cultures and customs are viewed by applying the concepts and values of one's own culture and an attitude of superiority prevents effective ministry. Biblical examples of ethnocentrism abound and should be analyzed for our profit. Consider Jonah and his attitude toward the pagan Ninevites. Deep cultural biases and the realization that Nineveh would someday be God's

---

1. Hiebert, *Anthropological Reflections*, 10.

instrument of chastisement on the Israelite people led Jonah to await their destruction even after their repentance (Jonah 4). We remember the apostles' astonishment in finding Jesus speaking with a female Samaritan libertine (John 4:9). The book of Acts records the struggle of the early church to break out from ethnocentrism. We find the dispute concerning the neglect of Greek-speaking Jews (6:1), Peter's reticence to go to Cornelius (10:28), Peter criticized by the circumcision party (11:3), and the Jerusalem Council which convened to arbitrate disputes that arose over implications of conversion for non-Jews (11:15).

Cross-cultural exposure and experience teach us how conditioned we are by our own culture. What we are and how we think reflects the influence of our ethnicity, gender, age, class, and educational advantages. It is easy to ignore the degree to which our own culture pervades our lifestyle and values. Even our approach and interpretation of Scripture and our positions on certain issues arise from the particularities of historical and cultural context. We should not insist that our way of living or viewpoints are necessarily superior to others unless they have been tested by the light of Scripture and are universal, timeless, and transcultural. Of course, the word of God alone is authoritative and our cultural conditioning does not prevent us, and those from other cultures, from rightly interpreting Scripture (2 Tim 2:15). The Christian church throughout the ages has spoken with one voice on the great doctrines of Scripture. Where we fail often is in the application of Scripture or in going beyond Scripture (1 Cor 4:6).

A monocultural and ethnocentric perspective arises partly from our view of culture. There are questions about culture we need to ask. Is culture basically a neutral vehicle through which God communicates to human beings? Or is culture inherently evil, created and contaminated by human beings and in need of transformation in light of a gospel perspective?[2] A response to this question may help us respond to other cultures, including our own, in a more realistic but not uncritical way. Monocultural myopia is tied to monoculturalism which itself has been understood in at least

---

2. Lingenfelter, *Transforming Culture*, 18.

three ways. "Eclectic monoculturalism" holds that through creative selection a superior culture has developed. "Reactionary monoculturalism" ridicules home cultures and glorifies other cultures. "One world monoculturalism" maintains that the world is becoming westernized, becoming like us. The proof is seen in the fact that Coca-Cola and McDonald's are found worldwide.[3]

The history of missions has seen a clash between different types of missionary activity including the colonial, anticolonial, and global models. We are indebted to our missionary forerunners and admire them for their heroism in blazing the gospel trail in hitherto unknown regions of the world. We ought to imitate their faith and avoid their mistakes just as we should want those who follow us to do the same. No generation should either uncritically accept the practices and paradigms of the past or quickly reject them by replacing them with what may prove to be novelties. Many of those who practiced colonial missions failed to see the distinction between the gospel and their culture. People were called not only to repentance but to deny aspects of their culture that defined their community and gave meaning to their existence, aspects which the gospel neither advocated nor condemned. Hiebert points out that the anticolonial reaction helped to differentiate between the gospel and culture but often led to theological relativism. The emphasis was one of dialogue and not proclamation of the saving gospel. The offense of the cross was sacrificed and evil unchallenged in the uncritical practice of contextualization.[4] A global perspective of missions reevaluates mission history, requires critical contextualization, and advocates an incarnational witness. This perspective also recognizes the variety of social environments and worldviews and subjects them all to the authority of Scripture.[5]

We may reminisce about the former days of missions and regard with great admiration those heroes who by their courage and sacrifice remain a powerful example for us of what God can do through his redeemed people. Nostalgia for those past days must

---

3. Van Rheenen, *Biblical Foundations*, 103–5.
4. Hiebert, *Anthropological Reflections*, 64–65.
5. Hiebert, *Anthropological Reflections*, 59.

not prevent us from confronting new realities in a world that in many respects is more accessible than ever before. Political upheavals and immigration have brought the world to our doorstep. The technological revolution with ease of travel and communication enables us to go to regions and peoples previously beyond our reach. Along with dramatic shifts in demographics, missions and ministry will never be the same. A few decades ago evangelicalism was basically confined to North America and Western Europe. It has been estimated that now 70 percent of the world's four hundred million evangelicals are non-Western. The greatest growth is now taking place in Asia and Africa.[6]

As new theologies are developed or old ones restated, North America and Western Europe will no longer dictate to the Christian world its views or perspectives without entering into constructive dialogue with non-Western believers as co-sojourners and as equal partakers of the grace of God. Third-world theologians must be heard and their concerns addressed. We reserve the right to agree or disagree but withdrawal and isolation are not viable options for Christians called to proclaim a gospel that is both global and absolute in its demands. It will not do to pretend that we have nothing to learn from non-Westerners. Some may fear theological relativism which is a great danger. An absolute allegiance to Scripture, an infallible and authoritative book, will guard us from error. Neither theological relativism nor theological stagnation are options.

On a practical level, now that we co-exist with people from other cultural backgrounds in our own communities and even in our churches, we need to understand what is good in other cultures. As Christians we can recognize positive elements of other cultures without embracing or dismissing them. The United States is becoming a nation of minorities and immigrants. If they are to be reached with the gospel, we must understand them and their felt needs, yet emphasize their real need of the only Savior, the Lord Jesus Christ. While we approach others with superior truth claims, (i.e., the uniqueness of Christ and the Christian

---

6. Lawton, "Faith Without Borders," 39–49.

Scriptures, salvation by grace through faith alone), we must not confront them from a standpoint of cultural superiority that arises from our monoculturalness. We must act in faithfulness to Scripture, refusing to be bound by cultural conventions that are neither biblical nor transcultural. Monocultural myopia becomes monocultural madness when it views the missionary task as finished or secondary to other concerns of the church. God desires to be worshiped by all people groups in diverse cultures in order to display the richness of his multi-faceted splendor. He calls us to participate in what he is doing among the peoples. For him, there are not the categories of Westerners and non-Westerners. There are only the saved and unsaved, worshipers in spirit and truth and non-worshipers. He does not call non-Westerners to become like us but to become like Christ in order that we may grow together into the fullness of Christ.

―――― Chapter 14 ――――

African Traditional Religion

My interest in Africa, its people, and its religions is rooted in the tremendous impact of the gospel on that continent, the great challenges to planting sound, biblical churches, the ravages of the false Prosperity Gospel, and the opportunity I've had to teach in Cameroon for several years. Recent statistics show that "Christianity is growing faster in Africa than any other place in the world and more Christians live in Africa than any other continent."[1] The independence of former colonies, the global struggle for racial equality, and efforts of decolonization have forced many mission agencies to relinquish ecclesiastical dominance. Many African churches have shaken off foreign control and have arrived at maturity in fruitful partnership with their Western counterparts. African Christians "want (and deserve) to work with the church in the Western world as coequals in the gospel for the cause of global missions."[2]

In the furtherance of the gospel in Africa, one of the common issues faced by Western partners and indigenous churches is African Traditional Religion (ATR). Any approach to ATR must take into account a number of factors. One's theological pre-commitments may influence how ATR is viewed and how the gospel will relate to it. Not only is there disagreement as to whether we should speak of ATR in the singular or plural but also what impact

1. Earls, "Encouraging Trends," para. 3.
2. Young, "White Rule," para. 18.

the gospel message will have in an African context, not only in behavior and beliefs but more significantly in worldview. A number of questions are posed: Do African religions contain sufficient revelatory and salvific truth so that the gospel simply adds a new dimension to what is already known? Or are the seeds of paganism and idolatry so deeply rooted in these religions so as to make necessary a complete uprooting of traditional aspects of religion including ritual observances at a surface level and worldview at a deeper level? The answers are complex and all approaches may be subject to criticism at some level. For example, those who find great value in ATR may err to the extreme of syncretism, "the view that there is no unique revelation in history, that there are many different ways to reach the divine reality."[3] Syncretism incorporates unbiblical elements that in effect make Christianity subject to culture and tradition. Others who advocate total change and find nothing of value in traditional African religions may be guilty of overthrowing the richness of African culture only to replace it with Western culture. There are undeniable communal and familial emphases rooted in ATR that do speak to Western individualism. A total abandonment of these and other values, and subsequent substitution of Western values, may result in a Christianity that is foreign, imposing practices or new patterns of thought that separate new converts from their own people and culture, ultimately hindering Christianity from being firmly and securely rooted in the consciousness of believers.

Two representative approaches will be used to illustrate the conceptual differences regarding African religions. Representing a broader, theologically liberal approach is the Kenyan, John S. Mbiti. Mbiti has been rightly called the "father of African theology." No one doing theology or missiology in an African context can ignore the impact and contribution of Mbiti. His stature as a serious theologian has been recognized by those of different theological stripes. A prolific writer, his writings include *African Religions and Philosophy, Concepts of God in Africa, Introduction to African Religion, Prayers of African Religion* and *New Testament Eschatology in*

3. Anderson, *Christianity and World Religions*, 17.

an African Background. Representing an evangelical approach are Nigerians, Byang Kato and Tokunboh Adeyemo, the former having written *Theological Pitfalls in Africa* and *Biblical Christianity in Africa*, the latter *Salvation in African Tradition*.

If we as Westerners desire to understand the African context we need to reflect on what those who have lived in that context have observed and experienced. Obviously we will filter what we read through our theological and cultural grids. Yet we can no more expect Westerners to adequately explain the African mind any more than we would expect a sub-Saharan African to understand and explain Western thought without adequate and prolonged exposure. This does not assume that African or Western thought is monolithic or incapable of being understood by those from outside the tradition. Our shared humanity implies an ability to communicate and to understand one another at some significant level. It merely asserts that those who have lived in both cultures may be valuable instructors.

Byang H. Kato (1936–1975) was born in Nigeria, raised in tribal religion, and became a Christian at a young age. His ministry training included Dallas Theological Seminary from which he graduated with both the S.T.M and Th.D. degrees. He served in a number of leadership positions in African-related religious organizations until his death in 1975.[4] Tokunboh Adeyemo (1944–2010) was born into a Muslim family and converted to Christianity in 1966. Formally educated at a Quranic school in Arabic, he memorized the Quran over a three-year period. He served as the General Secretary of the Association of Evangelicals in Africa.[5] John S. Mbiti (1931–2019) was a prolific writer and held various positions of influence and leadership including the directorship of the Ecumenical Institute of the World Council of Churches in Bossey, Switzerland and a professorship at Mdkere University in Uganda.[6]

---

4. Manana, "Kato," para. 2.
5. Manana, "Adeyemo," para. 2.
6. Oborji, "Mbiti," para. 5.

Tokunboh Adeyemo, in his preface to the 1996 edition of *Salvation in African Tradition*, states that "the battle for the survival of Biblical Christianity will be won or lost on the battlefield of soteriology."[7] The writer of the foreword, Gottfried Osei-Mensah, insists that "those who are tempted to look back longingly to the African past in hope of finding an authentic African way of salvation are warned that our forefathers knew no such way."[8] These statements succinctly summarize and put in perspective the debate between liberal and evangelical theologians. The question is not whether there is any value in African religions and traditions but whether or not they lead to salvation. ATR advocates see in Islam, Christianity, and ATR a "meeting point, somewhere, somehow, someday."[9] Adeyemo decries the fusion of Christianity and tradition evident in second generation Christians and rites of passage that detract from the uniqueness of Christ, and he criticizes "African theologians [who] have asserted that Jesus came to fulfill not only the Old Testament but the African traditional expectations."[10] Byang Kato fears the inroads of universalism in Africa.[11] He rejects the concept of an African theology understood in the sense that "it presupposes the validity of God's direct revelation to the worshipper of African religions."[12] Such an affirmation would make salvation possible through African religions apart from the uniqueness of Christ.

Mbiti was a brilliant thinker and makes many insightful observations based on his study of ATR. Although he overstates the value or closeness of some ATR thought to biblical teachings, he does not gloss over differences between ATR and Christianity. He recognizes that "African peoples do not 'thirst after God' for his own sake. They seek to obtain what he gives."[13] He observes

7. Adeyemo, *African Tradition*, 8.
8. Adeyemo, *African Tradition*, 7.
9. Adeyemo, *African Tradition*, 12–13.
10. Adeyemo, *African Tradition*, 28.
11. Kato, *Theological Pitfalls*, 11.
12. Kato, *Theological Pitfalls*, 54.
13. Mbiti, *Concepts of God*, 219.

that "these traditional religions cannot but remain tribal and nationalistic since they do not offer for mankind at large a way of 'escape,' a message of redemption."[14] According to Mbiti, most Africans do not expect any judgment after death. He mentions some exceptions then states that for "the majority of African peoples the hereafter is only a continuation of life more or less as it is in human form."[15] Adeyemo believes that this helps to account for the reception of the social gospel in Africa due to the African worldview emphasis on the abundant life.[16]

According to Kato, Mbiti has an overly positive view of ATR:

> After reading [Mbiti's] book, *Concepts of God in Africa*, one cannot but wonder what missionaries came to do in Africa. The book may be rightly called *A Systematic Theology of African Traditional Religions*, for these religions furnish the only source of information of his theology. The Bible becomes almost superfluous in the face of such a comprehensive work. African understanding of God seems to be complete and does not need any further light from elsewhere.[17]

Kato further asserts that Mbiti "has assumed the full revelation of God and the worship of that God through African traditional religions."[18] For Kato, it is possible to speak of African people having vestiges of the *imago Dei* with an awareness of the Supreme Being's existence. What he opposes as contrary to biblical Christianity are attempts to systematize these concepts and affirm that through them there is worship of the true God.[19] Kato warns that it is Mbiti's "universalism that poses a threat to Biblical Christianity in Africa" and asserts that "in a neo-orthodox fashion Mbiti hides his universalism by employing conservative evangelical language."[20]

14. Mbiti, *African Religions*, 128–29.
15. Mbiti, *African Religions*, 211.
16. Adeyemo, *African Tradition*, 64.
17. Kato, *Theological Pitfalls*, 69.
18. Kato, *Theological Pitfalls*, 70.
19. Kato, *Theological Pitfalls*, 75.
20. Kato, *Theological Pitfalls*, 57.

Kato believes that Mbiti's theology suffers greatly from his assertions of the African understanding of time as being circular or two-dimensional rather than linear time with a three-dimensional past, present, and future. Africans, according to Mbiti, cannot conceive of a distant future and thus have not understood the gospel message. Perhaps Mbiti can be criticized for his omissions as well. In his writings, while recognizing that ATR is not redemptive, it is not clear that he is convinced that salvation is in Christ alone, by faith alone. The lofty concepts and noble ideals of ATR are treated without suggesting that the cross provides the answer for the deepest need of Africans, indeed of all mankind, the forgiveness of sins through the blood of God's final sacrifice. His own theology radically spiritualizes concepts of heaven, hell, the new heaven and earth and he clearly believes in baptismal regeneration.[21]

This cursory overview cannot treat the many divergences which exist between evangelical and liberal perspectives of ATR. Evangelicals may affirm that ATR contains noble principles and insights that can be seen as vestiges of revealed truth. Time and decay, however, have distorted even these and ATR cannot be used as a trustworthy theological foundation. For that we must turn to Scripture as our final and only authority. Religious propositions that spring from sin-darkened minds and lead to a Christless eternity should never be elevated to the level of special revelation. ATR may possess certain moral truths and a call for high ideals. Yet we are not called to merely recognize non-life giving kernels of truth but to proclaim Christ as the Way, the Truth, and the Life. To do otherwise would be criminal in light of Christ's sacrifice for sin and of coming judgment. We owe to followers of ATR the respect due to their ways and traditions and should seek to familiarize ourselves with their religions. We should be willing to listen. But our irenicism and appreciation for certain aspects of ATR must never lead to an unwillingness to boldly herald the truth of God's word nor detract from our insistence on the superiority of Jesus Christ as the only confident hope of salvation.

---

21. Mbiti, *New Testament Eschatology*, 67–69.

——— Chapter 15 ———

Polygamy in Africa

For the past several years I have had the opportunity to teach pastors in Cameroon. During my time there I've visited different regions of the country. One memorable moment was meeting a tribal king in northern Cameroon. Although Cameroon has an elected government, hereditary dynasties which pre-dated colonialism continue to exercise influence over their tribes. Their lifestyle and privileges reflect their position of authority. Many of them also work tirelessly for the betterment of their people. This particular king, who will remain unnamed, invited our group to a meal prepared by one of his wives at his primary residence. Our conversation soon turned to his kingship, his ancestors, and his extended family. He was somewhat coy about how many wives he had and did not know how many children he had. We were told that he did not count his own children because all the village's children were considered his in order to not discriminate between biological offspring and non-biological children. He did not know he would be king until his father died. Now as king, he did not even know who his successor would be since the decision was made by elders and not announced publicly until the death of the king. He provided for multiple wives in different houses throughout his regional kingdom. We had the privilege of speaking to him about Christ, the gospel, and salvation. His religious background included Roman Catholicism, introduced during the colonial period, which had mixed with his ancestral religion to produce a syncretistic religion. We have remained in touch with him since that first meeting, mostly through WhatsApp and email, have sent gifts for his birthday and special events, and hope to see him again. One question in my mind concerned his multiple wives. What should he do if he became a Christian? What would his responsibility be toward his wives? Could he become a candidate for baptism and church membership? These are not easy questions and most Christians will never have to provide answers.

Any discussion of polygamy in an African context will often lead to immediate and heated debate and reaction from many sides. From the West in particular might come a myopic, moralistic response which views and dismisses polygamy as a pagan practice with neither biblical support (even if there is biblical precedent) nor place in a civilized society. A combination of abstract reasoning, archaic anthropological findings and natural law theory are often used to buttress the traditional viewpoint without considering concrete concerns and sociological implications. Monogamy is presented not only as the preferred marital state but also often imposed by missionaries as a condition for baptism and church membership when working among tribal peoples. Keep in mind that "only 20 percent of the world's ethno-linguistic people groups hold monogamy as the only possibility."[1] Those who practice polygamy are sometimes viewed as concupiscent and in search of satisfaction for their carnal cravings. To suggest otherwise might be viewed as a subterfuge to justify condemnable practices or to recommend the status quo in tribal sodalities over against change. This chapter simply seeks to hear the other side, neither justifying polygamy nor reducing the problem to ivory tower reasoning.

At the outset it might be helpful to clarify some terms. We in the West invariably use the word "polygamy" as a general catchall for the practice of having multiple wives. This is the situation with which we are most familiar. More precisely we should differentiate between "polygyny" and "polyandry." The former entails having multiple wives, the latter multiple husbands. When we speak of polygamy in a popular sense we usually mean polygyny

---

1. Kraft, *Anthropology*, 306.

since polyandry, or multiple husbands, "is exceedingly rare."[2] In this chapter, polygamy is employed in the popular sense of multiplicity of wives or simultaneous polygamy (as opposed to consecutive polygamy).

Some would liken the church's relation to polygamy in our day among first generation converts to the situation of the early church and her seeming toleration or accommodation of slavery. Were slave owners allowed to be baptized church members (i.e., Philemon)? Did Paul and other apostles seek to immediately overthrow this and other cultural givens that, while they may be considered sub-Christian, could not be easily or immediately suppressed without irreparable harm done to rooted, affinal structures? Notwithstanding the significant differences between first-century slavery and slavery practices in America, were southern Christian slave owners in America either refused church membership or disciplined because of their participation in the commercialization and exploitation of fellow bearers of the *imago Dei*? Why do we hold to a higher standard those who today practice an unacceptable custom and refuse to allow the persuasion of time and teaching to encourage them in the direction of monogamy? In all fairness, may polygamy be tolerated for those who enter into this state prior to conversion, and polygamists allowed baptism and church membership in order to participate at some level in the life of the church and communion at the Lord's Table? Or is the polygamous man required to divorce all but one wife (even though divorce in our culture might result in exclusion from church membership)?

Wherever the gospel is preached and polygamous sinners converted some have proposed that there must be an immediate cessation of such anti-Christian practices and the establishment of a monogamous relationship. What matters is doing what is considered right according to outsiders' cultural and perceived biblical norms. This may lead to divorcing all but the first wife or the preferred wife. Or it may lead to the economic maintenance of all wives and marital relationships with only one. Tragically, this position might lead the abandoned wives into prostitution. The complexity

2. Brooks, "Problem with Polygamy," 114.

of the problem becomes evident when we understand that we are dealing with people, not merely an ideal, and that upheaval in societal structures may lead to many unimagined consequences, some of which may be worse than polygamy itself. Polygamy becomes a missiological concern with vast implications for those involved in cross-cultural ministry. Pre-packaged responses from a Western perspective that theoretically resolve the tension may provide little guidance when confronted with the real world. Missionaries must have answers that are biblical and workable. They must not unwittingly condone practices that demand change nor condemn out-of-hand what they do not understand.

At this point a disclaimer must be made. I neither advocate polygamy for the monogamous nor the uncritical acceptance of the status quo in polygamous societies. All cultures and practices must come under the scrutiny of Scripture without yielding to naïve romanticism. I will argue for greater sensitivity in encountering these situations and the refusal to propose easy answers that prove not only unworkable but calamitous. This approach recognizes that our initial culturally-conditioned response may be neither the best nor biblical. The tendency is to judge rather than to reflect or to propose opinions or interpretations that have been flavored by our Western cultural perspective and, may I say, our sense of superiority in our relation to non-Westerners, i.e., the uncivilized.

Why would a happily married, monogamous male even entertain thoughts about the theoretical legitimacy of polygamy? Most of us will never have to wrestle with this problem except from our armchairs and within a constructed socio-cultural context that works well for us. Yet there are many who have faced and will confront this problem in other contexts as they seek to minister among those peoples where polygamy is not only tolerated but embraced. Only naïve realists will dismiss any possible divergence from their long held and cherished views while proffering arguments that ignore the corpus of Old Testament scriptures that appear to tolerate polygamy as seen in the lives of Abraham, David, and Solomon. It is significant that African Christians give greater place to the Old Testament since "there are great similarities between the Old Testament and African life in social structures and in such obvious matters as polygamy."[3] We should also keep in mind that many places where polygamous practices continue are pre-industrial, agricultural societies. Children are often valued more for what they contribute to household work and are cheaper than slaves. There is also the issue of high infant mortality. Unmarried women appear as a burden since they are not bearing children and do not have the physical strength for work traditionally done by males. Singleness and barrenness in many societies marginalize women who are considered, along with orphans and widows, as unable to contribute to household needs. They are simply another mouth to feed.

While God did not sanction polygamy, he did regulate it according to Deuteronomy 21:15: "If a man has two wives, one loved and the other unloved. . . ." God also regulated divorce (Deut 24:1), although Jesus taught that God allowed it because of the hardness of his people's hearts (Mark 10:4–6). Polygamy cannot be described as a divine institution but as a human convention. The Old Testament does not hide the downside of polygamy and the grief it brought into many families including those of the patriarchs. There are harmful effects of polygamy today including greater prevalence of sexual diseases among women in polygamous marriages, a higher incidence of behavioral and developmental problems among children from polygamous marriages, and higher levels of alcoholism among polygamous men.[4] And before we say that any man who has more than one wife deserves the misery he reaps, it might be helpful to consider that some men might become polygamous through the insistence of their first wife wanting help with domestic chores and agricultural tasks. Keep in mind that we are not speaking here of running the vacuum or dusting the furniture, concerns that few African women in tribal communities would have.

In the era of colonial missions during the eighteenth and nineteenth centuries, and to a large extent in the present era of global

---

3. Rieber, "Traditional Christianity," 271.
4. Brooks, "Problem with Polygamy," 112.

missions, there has been a quasi-united voice on how to deal with polygamous converts to Christianity. They would not be received for baptism and church membership as long as they remained in a polygamous relationship. They may be allowed to attend church services as second-class Christians but not admitted to the Lord's Table. Only by putting away all but the first wife could they be baptized and admitted into full fellowship in the church. And unmarried Christians who later opted for polygamy would be excluded from church membership. Polygamy has thus been viewed as "fundamentally inconsistent with the teaching of Christianity."[5]

The strength of this position is its desire to be faithful to the New Testament teaching of Christ concerning the ideal marital state in Matthew 19:3–9. Although given in the context of divorce, Christ reinforced the creation ideal of one man and one woman for life. Not only did God oppose divorce, allowing for it only because of the hardness of hearts, but he established the pattern for an indissoluble "one flesh" relationship between a man and a woman. These truths are incontrovertible for those who have a high view of the authority of Scripture. Alan Tippett expands on possible missionary responses to polygamy: (1) Baptism would be allowed for the converted wife and children of a polygamist but not the husband; (2) No one could be baptized who belonged to a polygamous household; (3) All could be baptized as a testimony to faith in Christ regardless of marital inconsistencies; (4) The polygamous husband must divorce all but his first wife; (5) As a variation on the fourth, the polygamous man must divorce all but the preferred wife, first or not.[6]

We might ask ourselves why there are dissonant voices today on the question of polygamy. One answer may be the contribution of the social sciences, especially anthropology, which have informed our understanding of "primitive" societies and reshaped the way we think about other cultures. This leads some who study foreign cultures and practices to contend that polygamy is "an indispensable socio-economic institution and a

5. Muthengi, "Polygamy and the Church," 57.
6. Tippett, "Polygamy as Missionary Problem," 75–79.

cultural ideal."[7] Others compare polygamy with the practice of having mistresses in Western culture although "adulterous affairs are most often performed secretly and hidden from the public's gaze whereas polygamous marriages are publicly recognized."[8] A framework faithful to Scripture does not ignore cultural ideals but neither can it obviate the scriptural teaching as to God's ideal. What may be viewed as indispensable and a societal ideal does not imply divine sanction or the inability or undesirability of change. Cultural romanticism must not detract from biblical reflection which leads to cultural transformation.

So why does polygamy flourish in many African societies? Can we not at least understand some of the dynamics at work in polygamous societies? Economics play a great part in subsistence societies where people live off the land. More wives and more children means more workers to labor in the fields. This may lead to situations where a first wife seeks relief from her toil by finding a second wife for her husband. It has also been observed that there are more marriageable women than men. This may be true not only because of natality and warfare but because men marry at a later age than women. Men need more time in order to acquire the material possessions necessary to sustain a household and to be able to afford bride-wealth. As an aside it needs to be said that an African does not buy a bride. According to Magesa "bride-wealth is not so much an economic transaction as it is a social and ritual symbol" and a "marriage solemnized with bride-wealth becomes a profoundly sacred reality."[9] There are many marriageable young girls who risk not finding a mate if they do not marry someone who already has a wife. Since children are the greatest African treasure, a woman does not want to remain unmarried and bear the shame of childlessness. Forced continence also plays a role. As one observer remarks: "A husband used to sex does not easily bear the intermittent celibacy

---

7. Hillman, "Polygyny Reconsidered," 60.
8. Brooks, "Problem with Polygamy," 110.
9. Magesa, *African Religion*, 131, 135.

of eighteen months or two years imposed by the old African avoidances during pregnancy and lactation."[10]

In the case of a barren first wife, a second wife compensates for the first wife's inability to bear children. A man desires descendants to carry on his name and to be remembered as an ancestor after his death.[11] Parrinder observed that "the ancestors are prayed to by the children, and many a woman prays, like Rachael, 'give me children or I die.' This desire to multiply and replenish the earth is one of the root reasons for polygamy and it has ensured the perpetuation of the race in times of high mortality."[12] In Western society childlessness may cause distress but there are medical means to address the problem, means not readily available in Africa. Also, in the West childlessness does not carry the same stigma felt by a childless African woman. "To be childless is to be cut off from the continuity of life, to be a 'dead-end.' Not only does one's life then lack significance, one also has failed the ancestors who were counting on descendants to enhance their heritage. . . . This importance of children is one reason given for the practice of polygamy."[13] We could also include the practice of levirate marriage where a man inherits the wife of a deceased brother in order to raise up children to carry on the deceased's name (Gen 38:8–10, Deut 25:5; Matt 22:24). These may not be adequate or biblical reasons for present day practice. Yet we need to try to understand the "why" of these practices before we can ever hope to propose a solution other than thoughtless condemnation and unrealistic demands. We must not forget that divorce forces a women to abandon her family, sometimes her children, and may lead her to prostitution as her only means of survival.[14]

So what do I tell my new friend the king if he becomes a Christian? Any argumentation, even with disclaimers and possible misrepresentation, seems to condone, overlook, or encourage

10. King, *Religions of Africa*, 76.
11. Kraft, *Anthropology*, 307.
12. Parrinder, *African Traditional Religion*, 61.
13. Booth, "Kasongo Niembo," 40.
14. Hillman, "Polygyny Reconsidered," 61–62.

polygamy, and will be rejected by many. Others may see the wisdom of refusing easy answers until the right questions have been raised. From a scriptural viewpoint we can demonstrate God's creation ideal of monogamy. Progressive revelation will not allow us to base our practice merely on what God allowed, regulated, or tolerated in the Old Testament economy. With patience in encountering engrained traditional practices, missionaries must accept the task to patiently teach, model, and affirm God's ideal. If there are polygamists admitted into the church they should affirm this ideal and not advance polygamy. For a time missionaries might need to tolerate what they cannot affirm and trust that the entrance of the gospel in all societies, in all traditions, will progressively bring conformity to biblical teaching and standards.

The directives and qualifications for an overseer found in 1 Timothy 3:1–7, especially "the husband of one wife," have received much attention and multiple interpretations. Kraft sees this as a prohibition against "digamy," remarriage after the death or divorce of one's wife and relates this to the Greek ideal that "marriage to one's wife is for eternity. . . . A person, especially a leader, should only marry once and not remarry if his wife dies or leaves him."[15] Even if this interpretation were correct and polygamy is not in view, a polygamous man admitted to church membership, in this writer's opinion, should not be allowed to accede to a position of church leadership. This would be necessary as an example for the next generation and to reinforce the scriptural ideal and preferred pattern for monogamy. The matter cannot be neatly solved. It remains to see how patient we can be with sub-biblical worldview issues but we should be no less patient than God. An inflexible position may prevent us from working toward the divine ideal and exclude multitudes from hearing gospel claims. We can be no more tolerant than God, nor more intransigent. God can work through his emissaries to bring societal transformation. It may not be immediate, but it will be no less radical and beneficent for seekers of truth.

---

15. Kraft, *Anthropology*, 306.

Chapter 16

Community and Individualism in the Church

LIVING IN POST-COMMUNIST ROMANIA in the mid-1990s was an incredible eye-opening experience. Communist control of religion and persecution of believers had bound Christians together in their church communities. Under communist rule, churches had been permitted to gather, albeit with restrictions, and pastoral training was allowed for only a few pastors. We were living in France in 1989 when communism began to unravel. We watched as the Berlin Wall fell and was dismantled in November. Freedom fever spread throughout Eastern Europe to Poland, Hungary, Bulgaria, and Czechoslovakia. Communist dictators were deposed, mostly by peaceful means, except in Romania. In December 1989, the brutal Romanian dictators Nicolae and Elena Ceaușescu were arrested after failing to stop an uprising. A brief trial followed after which they were lined up against a wall and summarily executed on Christmas Day.

With a new government in place, Romanian churches were allowed greater freedom to gather, and gather they did. In all kinds of weather, in the midst of political instability and uncertainty, they gathered with their church family. The cynical part of me says that they did this because they had little else to do. True, in the villages where we worked, Romanians rarely had phones, no cable TV, no internet, few distractions, and little to amuse them. What they did have were hard lives of manual labor, beaten down by years of oppression, and they had their church. We were often amazed at the faithfulness of God's people as they slogged through the mud on unpaved village roads to spend hours together for church services. In the summer, the church buildings were too hot. Windows were kept closed to avoid what they thought were unhealthy, sickness-producing breezes. In the winter, the buildings were heated by a pot belly stove in the middle of the church. No coat racks were needed because everyone was bundled up. I often preached not only in a suit but with an overcoat. The Christmas season was especially rich in time together—Christmas Eve morning, Christmas Eve, Christmas morning and evening, and the day after Christmas for good measure. On Christmas Day, visits were made to orphanages to take bags of candy and fruit to the children. Oranges were especially prized, and rare at that time. There was something about hardship which drew Christians together for fellowship and worship as often as possible. Romanian believers lived in community and had not yet discovered the radical individualism so rampant elsewhere. After several decades of freedom I'm not sure how much has changed for Christians in Romania. I don't want to suggest that community can only be found in times of oppression and persecution. Still, it makes one wonder if the freedoms we enjoy and the autonomous lives we live diminish the importance of community and how much we must fight for community in our liberal, open, and entertainment-driven societies.

Community might be defined as the interdependency of believers within the fellowship of faith where mutual love and encouragement flow freely and provide spiritual assistance to the multiple needs, problems, and crises faced by Christians. It is a sense of belonging to something larger than one's self. It also means that no Christian can expect to live out God's expectations for life and service apart from a constituted fellowship of believers, i.e., the local church. It is my opinion that many American Christians have accommodated the spirit of this age and are more in step with secular, hedonistic living than in living a faithful Christian life. Their pursuits are so out of sync with Scripture that they reap the inevitable whirlwind of their passions. How many

Christian parents begin trotting off their children to travel soccer on Sunday? How many believers jump at a job offer without considering if there is a good church to join? How many choose to work on Sunday when other options are available? I'm not talking about jobs that require Sunday work. Where would we be without police, firefighters, doctors, nurses, and a host of other professions who must work or be available at all times? My concern is more about an attitude, an indifference to the need of spiritual nurture and fellowship that keeps people from participating in the life of a Christian community.

Andrew Walls writes about the transition from communalism to individualism during the Reformation period and summarizes the introduction of radical individualism in Western society. This extreme form of individualism has found its place in the lives of many Christians and extends into the corporate life of the church, where the times with God's people are more and more rare, where other activities crowd already-busy schedules, and where sporting events dominate the Lord's Day.

> A necessary feature of barbarian Christianity was communal decision and mass response. But Western thought developed a particular consciousness of the *individual* as a monad, independent of kin-related identity. Christianity in its Western form adapted to this developing consciousness, until the concept of Christian faith as a matter of individual decision and individual application became one of the hallmarks of Western Christianity.[1]

Walls further comments on this in the context of differing perceptions of reality and the influences that in a great measure determine how we think:

> For centuries now, people in the West have tended to think of self in terms of individuality. . . . It is a natural consequence of the style of thinking which starts 'I think; therefore I exist.' In many societies elsewhere the starting point might be rendered, 'I *belong*, therefore I exist.'[2]

---

1. Walls, *Missionary Movement*, 21.
2. Walls, *Missionary Movement*, 45.

COMMUNITY AND INDIVIDUALISM IN THE CHURCH

We sometimes hear that real community cannot be discovered without suffering which brings believers to look for resources outside themselves and leads to bonding with other believers. Of course few would desire suffering and persecution in order to bring about changes that would enable them to live according to God's revealed purposes. We might think that an understanding and application of scriptural principles would lead to community even if our experience testifies to the difficulty of finding it. Might it not be that our worldview hinders community, that individualism as an underlying assumption inhibits the seeking after and the participation in community? Stanley Grenz puts it this way: "Enlightenment optimism, coupled with the focus on reason, elevates human freedom. . . . The Enlightenment project understands freedom largely in individual terms."[3] This does not deny the importance of an individual relationship and response to God. Again, according to Grenz:

> One of the great gains of modernity has been the elevation of the individual human person, indicative of modernity. We must always keep in view the biblical focus on the God who is concerned about each person, the individual as personally responsible to God, and a salvation message that is directed to every human being.[4]

We must also consider that our reality, or perception of it, confronts us with the fact that we often live our lives isolated from a life-affirming community; that we seek inner strength that is insufficient to help us; that we turn to outer resources that disappoint us. Our focus becomes self-centered to the point that we expect God not only to meet our needs, but to do so in a predictable, programmatic way. We want a life that is smooth and secure. Many turn to eclectic psychology to find solutions to problems which are symptomatic of a disoriented life out of fellowship with God and his people. It does appear that history confirms the age-old observation that prosperity and its accompaniments are

---

3. Grenz, "Star Trek," 91.
4. Grenz, "Star Trek," 98.

not always conducive to spirituality, and that dependence on God is sometimes weakened in times of abundance. Yet we also have biblical and historical testimony of those who have learned to use riches for the service and glory of God. There will always be a real struggle to live godly lives when we are so easily distracted and so often amused. Our leisure times, necessary as they are for moments of refreshing, easily lead to laziness and spiritual flabbiness. A sports-crazed, hero-worshipping, consumer-driven society leads us to seek satisfaction which is ephemeral and to satisfy appetites that have been created or whetted in us through publicity and crass commercialism. Superficiality substitutes for substance and character becomes a rare commodity. In American suburbs "a man works in one place, sleeps in another, shops somewhere else, finds pleasure and companionship where he can, and cares about none of these places."[5] The ancient words of the apostle Paul resonate today: "For they all seek their own interests, not those of Christ Jesus" (Phil 2:21).

A lack of community leads to a loss of missional, God-ordained purpose for the individual and for the church. How can community be found in modern America and more specifically among believers? While the achievement of community among the suffering church is commendable, is that model the necessary one for the evangelical church in the West? Certainly God in his providence can bring America to the place of repentance and renewal that might be found only along the path of oppression and tyranny. Although many Americans see themselves as God's chosen people, Scripture offers no guarantees of security for the protection and preservation of the nation. Even Israel, God's chosen people, forfeited the privileges of the covenants through disobedience and failure. They failed to carry out God's purpose in revealing himself through a redeemed people whose lives had been transformed. I propose that the way true community is found is in the church's engagement in the purposes and priorities of God in the advance of the gospel "in season and out of season" (2 Tim 4:2). We will see this fleshed out in the final chapter. Finding

5. Oldenburg, *Great Good Place*, 4.

COMMUNITY AND INDIVIDUALISM IN THE CHURCH

and experiencing community will necessarily involve rethinking our assumptions concerning individualism which have become rooted in American life and in church tradition. The Bible does have an emphasis on the individual and personal faith in Christ. The danger is that this faith is often lived outside a living community of believers. Christians are bereft of the fellowship so badly needed as they live as pilgrims and strangers in this world and detached from what God is doing in the world.

We may be amazed at what will be accomplished in our personal lives and in our churches as we fall in step with God's larger purpose of bringing glory to himself through redeeming individuals from every people group on the face of the earth. Christians whose sole purpose in life is their own security, satisfaction, and significance will always lead lives of frustration with little or no impact made in the world around them. When we begin to understand that God's priority is not our comfort, our health, or our pleasure, we will then be able to take the first step to entering into God's heart for the world. We will begin to understand that our problems, sometimes magnified out of all proportion to their true importance, and I speak by experience, pale in comparison to the problem of those who are without Christ and who desperately need to hear our voice.

Many believers live the American dream all the while oblivious to the world's nightmare. How many come to the end of life's journey, look back and realize that no impact was made, no lives were changed through them as instruments of God's power? The only way to escape from the emptiness of life is to engage in the worldwide mission of God, to understand that God redeems sinners "to show forth the praises of him who has called them from darkness into his marvelous light" (1 Pet 2:9). Christians cannot live autonomous lives, disconnected from the church and her mission. Tite Tiénou's comments from an African context are applicable here.

> For Christ and the New Testament writers, the reality of the church is one of living solidarity, where everyone is his brother's keeper. This interdependence can be

diversely expressed in images such as that of the body or the family, and others. Whatever image we use to represent the church as a caring community, one thing is certain: the local church is where it all begins.[6]

God's people need to ask themselves serious questions about who they are in God's world and plan. They need to ask themselves how they spend their time, their money, and their Sundays. They need a biblical view of possessions which will allow them to navigate through the shoals of commercialism. They must refuse bland Christianity that cannot impact lives or society. They will then see the world as it really is, alienated from God and desperately in need of hearing the gospel, a word of forgiveness and new life in Christ. As Grenz exhorts,

> Instead of elevating the individual to the center, therefore, postmodern evangelicals must carve out a theology that integrates the human person into community. . . . In short, in our theologizing we must take seriously the reality of community as the context in which the individual is necessarily embedded.[7]

There is no substitute for a life of corporate and personal prayer and worship, fellowship with believers, and reaching out to those around us. We are called to follow Christ, not the fads and fancies of our day. Our perspective must be one that realizes that "Only one life will soon be past, only what's done for Christ will last." When we enter the world above, in the sense that we begin to understand the heart of God, we will reach out in love and mercy to those around us and begin to share in this joyful experience with fellow believers. We will understand that even though we may have needs to be met, our greatest need has been meet in coming to know the Son of God in a personal way and that we have been grafted into a new community, a new family in which we relate to others in a new way. We will always be individuals in community which demonstrates our God-endowed diversity.

---

6. Tiénou, "Church in African Theology," 163.
7. Grenz, "Star Trek," 98–99.

Yet we must not allow individualism to hinder community which destroys our harmony and interferes with our mission. The tension between individualism and community is real and must be faced. Lack of community deprives us of human flourishing and from experiencing a present taste of God's presence and blessing which we will enjoy forever.

―――― Conclusion ――――

A Final Plea for Missional Living

THE FIRST CHAPTER OF this book highlighted the primacy of evangelism and church planting in missions in the twenty-first century. Since not all Christians are vocational missionaries, what I hope to accomplish in this last chapter is a simple reflection on the necessity of churches and Christians adopting a missional stance toward those who are outside the church and who are in desperate need of an encounter with followers of Jesus Christ. This missional stance will look different for believers according to their vocation in life but will be the same in their engagement with God's mission in the world. Many churches are mission-minded. They love missions. They support missionaries, even if mostly overseas. They would agree with Bosch that "Christianity is missionary by its very nature, or it denies its *raison d'être*."[1] They even allow missionaries to plant churches in other places that reflect the culture and community in which missionaries live. Yet often they are not intentionally engaged in reaching people for Christ in their own communities. Missions becomes a program among many in churches who see themselves as senders in sending others rather than seeing the church as sent into the world.[2] Churches remain locked in a cultural time-warp, ignoring the enormous changes in our society and the challenges in reaching people for Christ with the gospel.

1. Bosch, *Transforming Mission*, 9.
2. Guder, *Missional Church*, 6.

A FINAL PLEA FOR MISSIONAL LIVING

The use of the word "missional" needs some clarification. There are multiple and evolving definitions of missional and there is much to criticize in what has been called the missional church movement. When someone hears the word "missional," if the word is at all familiar, there may well be a reflex which associates the word with one's own experience. For some, missional sounds too New Age or Emergent or associated with compromising social gospelers. DeYoung and Gilbert affirm their support of missional in the sense of being "conscious of how everything we do should serve the mission of the church" but also believe "we'd do better to speak of living as citizens of the kingdom, rather than telling our people that they build the kingdom."[3] In my opinion, their concerns are well-founded. There are many definitions, examples, and aberrations of missional. There is something in missional for everyone to dislike. There is also much to affirm. We must not lose sight of what is valid and valuable for ministry in being missional when understood as "being a missionary without ever leaving your zip code" and "being intentional and deliberate about reaching others."[4] Of course, I do not believe that every Christian is technically a missionary except perhaps in the general sense of witnessing. In my mind, it's like saying every Christian is a pastor if they engage in pastoral-like activities. I would not use the word missionary in the way quoted above but I understand what they're saying. In my mind, calling all believers missionaries diminishes the important distinction of missionaries who are called and sent by churches to "focus on making disciples and multiplying churches among unreached peoples and places."[5] It would be better to say that every Christian is on mission and a witness to the saving and transforming power of Jesus Christ and should intentionally be involved in what God is doing both in their local community and in other places.

Yet I care far less about the word missional itself than the importance of believers and the churches of Jesus Christ living in

---

3. DeYoung and Gilbert, *Mission of the Church*, 20–21.
4. Stetzer, *Missional Churches*, 19.
5. Platt, "We Are Not All Missionaries," 99.

obedience to the Great Commission (Matt 28:16–20), not only in sending others but in seeing themselves as sent by God into the world for his mission to make disciples. Far more important than the word missional is our understanding of the church's mission in light of God's mission in the world. Making disciples is God's mission given to the disciples by Jesus Christ before his ascension which leads us into our activity to evangelize, disciple new believers, and organize them into churches. Missions is simply what we do as God's people, through God's church, to accomplish God's mission, and missions without gospel proclamation is an abuse of the word.

To further understand what it means to be missional, we must distinguish between different phases in our collective history. Some of us still remember the days when Christian churches were dominant in North America, at the center of society so to speak, places of influence, and when the majority of people to whom the church spoke had elements of a Christian worldview or some exposure to Christianity. People of other faiths were known mostly at a distance. Other religions were less visible. We refer to this period as Christendom where people often spoke of a Christian nation, or at least a nation guided by Christian principles, and where a majority of its citizens identified with Christianity. Missional believers do not seek a return to an imaginary golden age. In reality, our nation never was Christian. What nation can call itself Christian where slavery was tolerated until a bloody war ended it, where the rights of the unborn have been negated, and where the divine institution of marriage has been redefined to accommodate moral decline?

Times have changed. We now live in another phase, in another place occupied by competing worldviews. Christianity now competes among other faiths for a place in our society. If Christianity was one time at the center of society it now occupies the fringes and has been marginalized. Much of Christianity itself has become nominal and more of a civic religion "which promotes a god without any definition and a generic faith that demands and

A FINAL PLEA FOR MISSIONAL LIVING

asks nothing of its followers."[6] Yet, "the end of Christendom allows the church to recognize that the gospel is distinct from Western culture."[7] The people we meet every day are less biblically aware and have had little exposure to what it means to be truly Christian. They have not been raised in a "Christian" environment and Christianity is simply one way among many. Although we possess the changeless gospel to confront a changing and troubled world, there is little contact with the culture at large. Preaching the gospel has come to mean Sunday morning sermons for the faithful. Many evangelical believers rarely or never talk to people about Jesus and their need for salvation. Christians "may practice many of the good things that have been confused with evangelism without ever arriving at the point of verbal proclamation. . . . Hospitality, social work, serving others, etc. are good accompaniments to evangelism, but there is no evangelism without a verbal proclamation of the gospel."[8]

I don't want to sound pessimistic but we should be realistic in admitting that we are not going to significantly change our culture. In 2006, although there were "more megachurches than anytime in our history, and more people attending church than ever before in America, the culture has not for the most part been changed."[9] We also face the reality that what has been called cultural Christianity is "practiced by more Americans than any other faith or religion."[10] We live in a culture that is increasingly hostile to the gospel, where evangelistic methods of yesteryear are rarely effective, where many Christians and churches have isolated themselves from society, and many unsaved people would be surprised to find out that they had Christian neighbors. Secular ideology dominates government and education, viewpoints contrary to a so-called progressive agenda and free speech are under attack. This is not the time to throw up our hands either in disgust or despair. Jesus is

6. Inserra, *Unsaved Christian*, 36.
7. Stetzer, *Missional Churches*, 19.
8. Davis, *Ongoing Evangelism*, 42.
9. Stetzer, *Missional Churches*, 17.
10. Inserra, *Unsaved Christian*, 13.

still building his church and the ultimate triumph is assured. God's people need to be on the offensive, with any offense or persecution coming from the gospel and not from our personal harshness or foolishness. We cannot be silent on the issues of our day which the Bible addresses—that people are lost and go to hell without Christ (Matt 25:46), that marriage is between a man and a woman (Gen 1:26–27, 2:24; Matt 19:4–6), that sexual activity outside of marriage, whether heterosexual or homosexual, is sin and brings one under the judgment of God (1 Cor 6:9–10; Heb 13:4). People have the right to reject Christ as Savior, to decide how they will live, and in our society choose who they will marry. But the church cannot affirm what God condemns. He will be the final judge. People need to be warned and choose wisely.

In a December 2021 Pew Forum report, research confirms that the "secularizing shifts evident in American society show no sign of slowing." Although Christians remain a majority, "their share of the adult population is 12 points lower in 2021 than it was in 2011."[11] Regions that were once safely considered "Bible Belt" are changing as more cities grow post-Christian, with more people who don't believe in God, who no longer attend church with any frequency, and who do not believe the Bible to be the authoritative word of God. In 2009, 82 percent of adults in the South self-identified as Christians compared to 70 percent today. Between 2007 and 2021 the number of self-identified born-again or evangelical Protestants in the United States dropped from 30 to 24 percent of the adult population.[12] These changes are consistent with a global shift of Christianity from the Global West to the Global South. Although "the percentage of the world that is Christian has changed very little over the last 120 years," there have been "dramatic changes in Christianity's demographics." In 1900 "82 percent of all Christians lived in Europe and North America; by 2020 this figure had dropped dramatically to 33 percent."[13]

---

11. Smith, "Three-in-Ten U.S. Adults," para. 2.
12. Etheridge, "Vanishing Bible Belt," para. 12.
13. Zurlo and Johnson, "Christianity Shrinking or Shifting," para. 6.

A FINAL PLEA FOR MISSIONAL LIVING

Christians and churches in North America might bear at least some of the responsibility for the present situation of the decline of Christianity. Many churches fled the cities over the last few decades to find suburban refuge, an exodus which slowed in 2020 during the COVID-19 pandemic.[14] While it is true that the Bible does not command the church to prioritize cities, cities are important economically and culturally with global connections.[15] The major influences of our society largely take place in cities where we find institutions of higher learning and government. As churches fled the cities, Christian influence waned as believers retreated from dark places in need of a gospel witness. Churches built large and impressive suburban ministries and campuses. These ministries were fed by a steady stream of Christians moving into the suburbs. Churches often grew from adding displaced Christians and most evangelism was done by bringing in evangelists for special meetings. Many churches started Christian schools to protect their children from ungodly influences in public schools. The importance of Christian education cannot be overemphasized. We need more, not fewer, Christian educational institutions. One downside of Christian education, however, has been reduced contact with nonbelievers and fewer Christian teachers in public schools. Of course, in some public school environments Christian teachers can no longer survive with their convictions intact due to a radical, progressive political agenda and hostility toward Christian viewpoints.

The past few years have seen many evangelicals' loyalty to a political party trump their allegiance to Christ and his church. We observe today that many Christians are ready to vocally defend their rights yet remain silent when it comes to calling people to repentance. Many people and groups associated with the Christian Right have become tools of political parties and many churches all too quickly jump on political bandwagons which further estrange them from their fellow-citizens. Evenings spent sitting in front of the television with heavy doses of cable news become

---

14. Fry and Cohn, "Exodus from Cities Slowed," para. 1.
15. Bergquist and Crane, *City Shaped Churches*, 47.

more formative than a once-a-week sermon. If Christians were as vocal in their Christian witness as they are in publicizing their political affiliation, there would be more opportunities to share the gospel. Partisan politics has become the hallmark of many churches which has created an enclave mentality cutting off believers from contact with outsiders. Important concerns like COVID-19 vaccines and masks have become central and contentious on all sides of the issues. Churches which were not supposed to be "of the world" are no longer truly "in the world." Christian subcultures have removed salt and light from society. Churches are seen as havens of refuge for Christians alienated from their communities. Churches began online services during COVID-19 and some Christians, apart from those immunocompromised, grew comfortable staying home out of either debilitating fear or convenience. Church attendance, already declining steadily over the past decade, dwindled even more during the pandemic. Statistics vary from region to region but "one-in-three practicing Christians dropped out of church completely during COVID-19."[16] The long-term results remain to be seen.

The present decline of Christian influence and a fortress mentality cannot be reversed overnight. There is no utopian redemption for our cities and our nation. There is no reversal for the moral decay and corruption of our society apart from divine intervention. But there is redemption and transformation of lives through the gospel of Jesus Christ. The furtherance of the gospel is what it means to be missional! There is hope for the hopeless, help for the helpless. Addictions are broken and families made whole. Believers become salt and light in government, in institutions of higher learning, in public schools, and in community organizations. God's answer for the sins and ills of our society is the gospel of grace. Churches know this but without engagement with the world, without returning to the dense and diverse populations of our cities, there is little reason to hope for substantive change. I do not know what engagement looks like for all churches, whether urban, suburban, or rural, all which have

---

16. Wang, "Decline in Church Attendance," para. 3.

A FINAL PLEA FOR MISSIONAL LIVING

a place in God's program. Churches need to determine that engagement in their place and time, with their resources, and with issues and needs facing their communities. The question remains the same: How can we represent our great God and the glorious gospel of Jesus Christ so that all within our reach might have the opportunity to hear the good news?

Christians and churches must commit to a missional engagement as the sent people of God in taking the gospel to those long ignored. They may need to break some of their addictions to this world and its comforts. As Piper remarks, "It's the people who know their hope, who know that their destiny is rock-solid and sure, who know their destiny is glorious, who are free to take risks of love, free to 'let goods and kindred go, this mortal life also. The body they may kill; God's truth abideth still.'"[17] Christians can begin to build redemptive relationships with outsiders or continue to fear contamination by association with strangers. They can continue to avoid addressing societal problems or they can raise a prophetic voice against evil in its variegated forms and seek to alleviate human suffering as a legitimate implication of transformative gospel ministry. They can continue to fight among themselves or they can turn their weapons of warfare to pull down enemy strongholds. They can continue to use their resources mostly to sustain their institutions and maintain the status quo or they can invest in planting new churches to reconquer cities and towns enveloped in darkness.

Many churches are not able to make the transition from being merely mission-minded, that is, caring about missions, to becoming radically missional. And thankfully, in spite of that, God in his good pleasure will deign to use them in his own way for his glory. Sadly, some of these churches will continue their decline as they remain unable or unwilling to engage the new realities of our day; some will continue to receive a stream or trickle of new members who were Christianized elsewhere and added to membership rolls. What our nation needs is churches to invest in advancing the gospel and planting faithful churches both at home and abroad,

17. Piper, "Escaping the Love of Comfort," para. 9.

effective in blending cross-cultural ministry and counter-cultural living. We are living in unusual and challenging times in uncharted territory. But we are kidding ourselves if we think that our situation is more desperate than the challenges faced by Christians in the past or that our situation is hopeless to the point of despair. Will we remain paralyzed in place with fear or will we faithfully go to Jesus who stands outside the camp (Heb 13:13)? We may find temporary safety behind the walls we construct but we need to peer over the edges and see where Jesus is, with the outsiders, and join him there. He's outside many lives and ministries which refuse to leave their comfort zones to encounter the world. God's word exhorts us to go unto Jesus bearing his reproach. By his grace may we be the missional people of God!

Bibliography

Adeyemo, Tokunboh. *Salvation in African Tradition*. 2nd ed. Nairobi: Evangel, 1977.
Allen, Roland. *Missionary Methods: St Paul's or Ours?* rev. ed. Cambridge: Luttherworth, 2006.
Aly, Götz. *Europe Against the Jews: 1880-1945*. Translated by Jefferson Chase. New York: Henry Holt, 2020.
Anderson, Elijah. *Code of the Street: Decency, Violence, and the Moral Life of the Inner City*. New York: W. W. Norton, 1999.
Anderson, Sir Norman. *Christianity and World Religions: The Challenge of Pluralism*. Downers Grove, IL: InterVarsity, 1984.
Ankerberg, John, et al. *The Facts on Islam*. Eugene, OR: Harvest House, 1992.
Barrett, David. *Schism and Renewal in Africa: An Analysis of Six Thousand Contemporary Religious Movements*. London: Oxford University Press, 1968.
Beilby, James. *Postmortem Opportunity: A Biblical and Theological Assessment of Salvation after Death*. Downers Grove, IL: IVP Academic, 2021.
Bennett, Matthew Aaron. *Narratives in Conflict: Atonement in Hebrews and the Qur'an*. Eugene, OR: Pickwick, 2019.
Bergquist, Linda, and Michael D. Crane. *City Shaped Churches: Planting Churches in the Global Era*. Skyforest, CA: Urban Loft, 2018.
Bevans, Stephen, et al. *The Mission of the Church: Five Views in Conversation*. Edited by Craig Ott. Grand Rapids: Baker Academic, 2016.
Blight, David W. *Frederick Douglass: Prophet of Freedom*. New York: Simon & Shuster, 2018.
Booth, Jr., Newell S. "The View from Kasongo Niembo." In *African Religions: A Symposium*. New York: NOK, 1977.
Bosch, David J. "An Emerging Paradigm for Mission." *Missiology* 10 (October 1983) 485-508.
———. *Transforming Mission: Paradigm Shifts in Theology of Mission*. Maryknoll, NY: Orbis, 1991.

BIBLIOGRAPHY

Brooks, Thom. "The Problem with Polygamy." *Philosophical Topics* 37 (Fall 2009) 109–22. http://www.jstor.org/stable/43154559.

Burge, Gary M. *Whose Land? Whose Promise? What Christians Are Not Being Told about Israel and the Palestinians.* Cleveland, OH: Pilgrim, 2003.

Carson, D. A. "How Do We Work for Justice and Not Undermine Evangelism?" *The Gospel Coalition* (October 18, 2010). https://www.thegospelcoalition.org/article/asks-carson-justice-evangelism/.

———. "What is the Gospel?" *The Gospel Coalition* (May 28, 2007). https://www.thegospelcoalition.org/conference_media/what-is-the-gospel/.

Casper, Jayson. "Trump or Netanyahu? American Evangelicals Support Israel, Yet signs of Change." *Christianity Today* (December 15, 2021). https://www.christianitytoday.com/news/2021/december/american-evangelicals-israel-palestinians-barna-survey-cpm.html.

Clark, Elliot. *Mission Affirmed: Recovering the Missionary Motivation of Paul.* Wheaton, IL: Crossway, 2022.

Combs, William W. "The Biblical Role of the Evangelist." *Detroit Baptist Seminary Journal* 7 (Fall 2002) 23–48.

Compton, Jared, and Andrew David Naselli, eds. *Three Views on Israel and the Church: Perspectives on Romans 9–11.* Grand Rapids: Kegel Academic, 2018.

Compton, R. Bruce. "First Corinthians 13 and the Cessation of Miraculous Gifts: A Critique of Thomas Schreiner's *Spiritual Gifts: What They Are and Why They Matter*." *Detroit Baptist Seminary Journal* 25 (2020) 31–49.

Corbett, Steve, and Brian Fikkert. *When Helping Hurts: How to Alleviate Poverty Without Hurting the Poor . . . and Yourself.* Chicago: Moody, 2012.

Corduan, Winfried. *Neighboring Faiths: A Christian Introduction to World Religions.* Downers Grove, IL: InterVarsity, 1998.

Corwin, Gary. "MissionS: Why the "S" is Important to Church Strategy." In *Conversations on When Everything is Missions*, edited by Denny Spitters and Matthew Ellison, 71–77. Albuquerque, NM: Pioneers-USA, 2020.

Daniels, Gene, and Warrick Farah, eds. *Margins of Islam: Ministry in Diverse Muslim Contexts.* Pasadena, CA: William Carey, 2018.

Davies, W. D. *The Gospel and the Land: Early Christianity and Jewish Territorial Doctrine.* Berkeley, CA: University of California Press, 1974.

Davis, John P. *Ongoing Personal Evangelism: Factors that Influence Evangelism.* Eugene, OR: Resource, 2021.

———. *Who are the Heirs of the Abrahamic Covenant?* Eugene, OR: Wipf & Stock, 2022.

Deressa, Samuel Yonas, ed. *Christian Theology in African Context: Essential Writings of Eshetu Abate.* Minneapolis: Lutheran University Press, 2015.

DeYoung, Kevin, and Greg Gilbert. *What is the Mission of the Church? Making Sense of Social Justice, Shalom, and the Great Commission.* Wheaton, IL: Crossway, 2011.

Dictionary of African Christian Biography. https://dacb.org/.

BIBLIOGRAPHY

Earls, Aaron. "7 Encouraging Trends of Global Christianity in 2022." *Lifeway Research* (January 31, 2022). https://lifewayresearch.com/2022/01/31/7-encouraging-trends-of-global-christianity-in-2022/.

Etheridge, Kristy. "The Vanishing Bible Belt." *Lifeway Research* (February 2, 2022). https://lifewayresearch.com/2021/02/03/the-vanishing-bible-belt-the-secrets-southern-churches-must-learn-to-stay-healthy/.

Ferguson, Sinclair. *The Dawn of Redeeming Grace: Daily Devotions for Advent.* Charlotte, NC: Good Book, 2021.

Fishbein, H. D. "The Genetic/Evolutionary Basis of Prejudice and Hatred." *Journal of Hate Studies* 3 (2004) 113–19. http://doi.org/10.33972/jhs.24.

Fry, Richard, and D'Vera Cohn. "In 2020, Fewer Americans Moved, Exodus from Cities Slowed." *Pew Research Center* (December 16, 2021). https://www.pewresearch.org/fact-tank/2021/12/16/in-2020-fewer-americans-moved-exodus-from-cities-slowed/.

Geivett, R. Douglas, and W. Gary Phillips. "A Particularist View: An Evidentialist Approach." In *Four Views on Salvation in a Pluralistic World*, edited by Dennis L. Okholm and Timothy R. Phillips, 211–70. Grand Rapids: Zondervan, 1996.

Gettleman, Marvin E., and Stuart Schaar, eds. *The Middle East and Islamic World Reader.* New York: Grove, 2003.

Grenz, Stanley J. "Star Trek and the New Generation: Postmodernism and the Future of Evangelical Theology." In *The Challenge of Postmodernism: An Evangelical Engagement,* edited by David S. Dockery, 75–89. Wheaton, IL: Victor, 1995.

Grosheide, F. W. *The First Epistle to the Corinthians.* The New International Commentary on the New Testament. Grand Rapids: Eerdmans, 1976.

Guder, Darrell L., ed. *Missional Church: A Vision for the Sending of the Church in North America.* Grand Rapids: Eerdmans, 1998.

Harris, R. Laird, et al. *Theological Wordbook of the Old Testament.* Vol. 1. Chicago: Moody, 1980.

Hart, Trevor. "Universalism: Two Distinct Types." In *Universalism and the Doctrine of Hell,* edited by Nigel M. de S. Cameron, 1–34. Carlisle, UK: Paternoster, 1992.

Herzog, Chaim. *The War of Atonement: The Inside Story of the Yom Kippur War.* New York: Skyhorse, 2018.

Hesselgrave, David J. *Communicating Christ Cross-Culturally.* 2nd ed. Grand Rapids: Zondervan, 1991.

———. *Planting Churches Cross-Culturally.* 2nd ed. Grand Rapids: Baker, 2000.

Hick, John. "A Pluralist View." In *Four Views on Salvation in a Pluralistic World,* edited by Dennis L. Okholm and Timothy R. Phillips, 27–92. Grand Rapids: Zondervan, 1996.

———. *Death and Eternal Life.* Louisville: Westminster, 1994.

Hick, John, and Paul Knitter, eds. *The Myth of Christian Uniqueness: Toward a Pluralistic Theology of Religions.* Maryknoll, NY: Orbis, 1987.

BIBLIOGRAPHY

Hiebert, Paul G. *Anthropological Reflections on Missiological Issues.* Grand Rapids: Baker, 1994.

Hillman, Eugene S. "Polygyny Reconsidered." *Practical Anthropology* 17 (March–April 1970) 60–74.

Hodge, Charles. *Systematic Theology.* Vol. 3. Grand Rapids: Eerdmans, 1968.

Hollinger, Dennis P. *Individualism and Social Ethics: An Evangelical Syncretism.* Lanham, MD: University Press of America, 1983.

Hume, David. *An Inquiry Concerning Human Understanding.* Oxford: Oxford University Press, 2007.

Inserra, Dean. *The Unsaved Christian: Reaching Cultural Christianity with the Gospel.* Chicago: Moody, 2019.

Kaemingk, Matthew. *Christian Hospitality and Muslim Immigration in an Age of Fear.* Grand Rapids: Eerdmans, 2018.

Kaiser, Jr., Walter C. "Jewish Evangelism in the New Millennium in Light of Israel's Future." In *To the Jew First: The Case for Jewish Evangelism in Scripture and History,* edited by Darrell L. Bock and Mitch Glaser, 40–52. Grand Rapids: Kregel Academic, 2008.

Kato, Byang H. *Biblical Christianity in Africa: Theological Perspectives in Africa.* Achimota, Ghana: African Christian, 1985.

———. *Theological Pitfalls in Africa.* Kisumu, Kenya: Evangel, 1975.

Kaufman, Gordon D. "Religious Diversity, Historical Consciousness, and Christian Theology." In *The Myth of Christian Uniqueness: Toward a Pluralistic Theology of Religions,* edited by John Hick and Paul F. Knitter, 3–15. Maryknoll, NY: Orbis, 1987.

Keener, Craig S. "Miracles are Outlasting the Arguments Against Them." *Christianity Today* (January 24, 2022). https://www.christianitytoday.com/ct/2022/january-web-only/craig-keener-miracles-today-supernatural-god.html.

———. *Miracles: The Credibility of the New Testament Accounts.* Grand Rapids: Baker Academic, 2011.

———. *Miracles Today: The Supernatural Work of God in the Modern World.* Grand Rapids: Baker Academic, 2021.

Keil, C.F., and F. Delitzsch. *Commentary on the Old Testament.* Vol. 10. Grand Rapids: Eerdmans, 1975.

Keller, Tim. "The Gospel and the Poor." *Themelios* 33 (2008) 8–22. https://www.thegospelcoalition.org/themelios/article/the-gospel-and-the-poor/.

———. *Ministries of Mercy: The Call of the Jericho Road.* 2nd ed. Phillipsburg, NJ: P&R, 1997.

King, Noel Q. *Religions of Africa: A Pilgrimage into Traditional Religions.* New York: Harper & Row, 1970.

Kistemaker, Simon J. *Exposition of the First Epistle to the Corinthians.* New Testament Commentary. Grand Rapids: Baker, 1993.

Köstenberger, Andreas J. "The Place of Mission in New Testament Theology." *Missiology* 27 (July 1999) 347–62.

BIBLIOGRAPHY

Kraft, Charles H. *Anthropology for Christian Witness*. Maryknoll, NY: Orbis, 1996.

———. *Christianity with Power: Your Worldview and Your Experience of the Supernatural*. Eugene, OR: Wipf & Stock, 2005.

———. *Dealing with Demons*. Eugene, OR. Wipf & Stock, 2018.

———. *Two Hours to Freedom: A Simple and Effective Model for Healing and Deliverance*. Grand Rapids: Chosen, 2010.

Kuiper, R. B. *For Whom Did Christ Die? A Study of the Divine Design of the Atonement*. Grand Rapids: Eerdmans, 1959.

———. *The Glorious Body of Christ: A Scriptural Appreciation of the One Holy Church*. Carlisle, PA: Banner of Truth, 1967.

Ladd, George Elton. *Presence of the Future: The Eschatology of Biblical Realism*. Grand Rapids: Eerdmans, 1996.

Lawton, Kim A. "Faith Without Borders: How the Developing World is Changing the Face of Christianity." *Christianity Today* 41 (May 19, 1997) 39–49.

Leeman, Jonathan. "Soteriological Mission: Focusing in on the Mission of Redemption." In *Four Views on the Church's Mission*, edited by Jason S. Sexton, 17–45. Grand Rapids: Zondervan, 2017.

Lindsell, Harold. *A Christian Philosophy of Missions*. Wheaton, IL: Van Kampen, 1949.

Lingenfelter, Sherwood. *Transforming Culture: A Challenge for Christian Mission*. Grand Rapids: Baker, 1992.

Lipka, Michael. "Muslims and Islam: Key Findings in the U.S. and Around the World." *Pew Research Center* (August 9, 2015). https://www.pewresearch.org/fact-tank/2017/08/09/muslims-and-islam-key-findings-in-the-u-s-and-around-the-world/.

Magesa, Laurenti. *African Religion: The Moral Traditions of Abundant Life*. Maryknoll, NY: Orbis, 1997.

Manana, Francis. "Adeyemo, Tokunboh." *Dictionary of African Christian Theology*. https://dacb.org/stories/nigeria/adeyemo-tokunboh.

———. "Kato, Byang Henry." *Dictionary of African Christian Theology*. https://dacb.org/stories/nigeria/kato-byang.

Mason, Eric, ed. *Urban Apologetics: Restoring Black Dignity with the Gospel*. Grand Rapids: Zondervan, 2021.

Mbiti, John S. *African Religions and Philosophy*. New York: Praeger, 1969.

———. *Concepts of God in Africa*. New York: Praeger, 1970.

———. *Introduction to African Religion*. New York: Praeger, 1975.

———. *New Testament Eschatology in an African Background*. London: Oxford University Press, 1971.

———. *The Prayers of African Religion*. Maryknoll, NY: Orbis, 1975.

McGrath, Alister. "A Particularist View: A Post-Enlightenment Approach." In *Four Views on Salvation in a Pluralistic World*, edited by Dennis L. Okholm and Timothy R. Phillips, 149–210. Grand Rapids: Zondervan, 1996.

Morris, Leon. *The Epistle to the Romans*. Grand Rapids: Eerdmans, 1988.

BIBLIOGRAPHY

Muthengi, Juliusk. "Polygamy and the Church in Africa: Biblical, Historical, and Practical Perspective." *Africa Journal of Evangelical Theology* 14 (1995) 55–78.

Newbigin, Lesslie. "Religious Pluralism and the Uniqueness of Jesus Christ." *International Bulletin of Missionary Research* 13 (April 1989) 50–54.

Oborji, Francis Anekwe. "Mbiti, John Samuel." *Dictionary of African Christian Theology*. https://dacb.org/stories/kenya/mbiti-johns/.

Okholm, Dennis L., and Timothy R. Phillips, eds. *Four Views on Salvation in a Pluralistic World*. Grand Rapids: Zondervan, 1996.

Oldenburg, Ray. *The Great Good Place: Cafes, Coffee Shops, Bookstores, Bars, Hair Salons, and Other Hangouts at the Heart of a Community*. New York: Marlowe & Company, 1999.

Palmer, Chris. "A Philly Committee Spent 18 Months Examining the City's Gun Violence Crisis." *Philadelphia Inquirer* (January 27, 2022). https://www.inquirer.com/news/philadelphia-gun-violence-homicides-report-city-council-20220127.html.

———. "Over 65 Shots Fired on Busy Philadelphia Street." *Philadelphia Inquirer* (December 31, 2021). https://www.inquirer.com/news/philadelphia-gun-violence-germantown-mass-shooting-20211231.html.

Panikkar, Raimundo. "The Jordan, the Tiber, the Ganges: Three Kairological Moments of Christic Self-Consciousness." In *The Myth of Christian Uniqueness: Toward a Pluralistic Theology of Religions*, edited by John Hick and Paul F. Knitter, 89–116. Maryknoll, NY: Orbis, 1994.

Parrinder, E. G. *African Traditional Religion*: London: SPCK, 1954.

Payne, J. D. "Currents of Change: How Did Everything Become Missions?" In *Conversations on When Everything is Missions*, edited by Denny Spitters and Matthew Ellison, 11–19. Albuquerque, NM: Pioneers-USA, 2020.

Peterson, David G. "Maturity: The Goal of Missions." In *The Gospel to the Nations: Perspectives on Paul's Mission*, edited by Peter Bolt and Mark Thompson, 185–204. Downers Grove, IL: IVP, 2000.

Pierson, Arthur T. *The Crisis of Missions:, or, The Voice out of the Cloud*. New York: Baker & Taylor, 1886.

Piper, John. "Christians Care About all Suffering and Injustice." *Desiring God* (August 25, 2019). https://www.desiringgod.org/messages/christians-care-about-all-suffering-and-injustice.

———. "Escaping the Love of Comfort and Safety." *Desiring God* (February 9, 2022). https://www.desiringgod.org/interviews/escaping-the-love-of-comfort-and-safety.

———. *Providence*. Wheaton, IL: Crossway, 2020.

Platt, David. "We Are Not All Missionaries, But We Are All on Mission." In *Conversations on When Everything is Missions*, edited by Denny Spitters and Matthew Ellison, 97–105. Albuquerque, NM: Pioneers-USA, 2020.

Pratt, Jr., Richard L. "To the Jew First: A Reformed Perspective." In *To the Jew First: The Case for Jewish Evangelism in Scripture and History*, edited

BIBLIOGRAPHY

by Darrell L. Bock and Mitch Glaser, 168–88. Grand Rapids: Kregel Academic, 2008.
Priest, Robert J., ed. *Effective Engagement in Short-Term Missions: Doing It Right!* Pasadena, CA: William Carey, 2008.
Rieber, Calvin. "Traditional Christianity as an African Religion." In *African Religion: A Symposium*, edited by Newell S. Booth, Jr., 255–74. New York: NOK, 1977.
Ross, Melanie C. *Evangelical Worship: An American Mosaic.* New York: Oxford University Press, 2021.
Ryrie, Charles C. *Dispensationalism Today.* Chicago: Moody, 1965.
Sanders, J. Oswald. *What of the Unevangelized?* London: Overseas Missionary Fellowship, 1966.
Sanders, John. *No Other Name: An Investigation into the Destiny of the Unevangelized.* Grand Rapids: Eerdmans, 1992.
Saucy, Robert L. "Israel and the Church: A Case for Discontinuity." In *Continuity and Discontinuity: Perspectives on the Relationship Between the Old and the New Testaments*, edited by John S. Feinberg, 239–58. Wheaton, IL: Crossway, 1988.
Schnabel, Eckhard J. *Paul the Missionary: Realities, Strategies and Methods.* Downers Grove, IL: IVP Academic, 2008.
Schwartz, Glenn. "Is There a Cure?" *Mission Frontiers* (March 1, 2001). https://www.missionfrontiers.org/issue/article/is-there-a-cure.
Shedd, William G. T. *A Critical and Doctrinal Commentary on the Epistle of St. Paul to the Romans.* Minneapolis: Klock & Klock, 1978.
Sheikh, Bilquis. *I Dared to Call Him Father: The Miraculous Story of a Muslim Woman's Encounter with God.* Bloomington, MN: Chosen, 2003.
Smietana, Bob. "Sunday Morning in American Still Segregated—and That's OK With Worshipers." *Lifeway Research* (January 15, 2015). https://lifewayresearch.com/2015/01/15/sunday-morning-in-america-still-segregated-and-thats-ok-with-worshipers/.
Smith, Gregory A. "About One-in-Ten U. S. Adults Are Now Religiously Unaffiliated." *Pew Research Center* (December 14, 2021). https://www.pewforum.org/2021/12/14/about-three-in-ten-u-s-adults-are-now-religiously-unaffiliated/.
Spitters, Denny, and Matthew Ellison, eds. *Conversations on When Everything is Missions.* Albuquerque, NM: Pioneers-USA, 2020.
Spitters, Denny, and Matthew Ellison. *When Everything is Missions.* Albuquerque, NM: Bottomline Media, 2017.
Steffen, Tom. *Passing the Baton: Church Planting that Empowers.* La Habra, CA: Center for Organizational & Ministry Development, 1997.
Stetzer, Ed. *Planting Missional Churches.* Nashville: B&H Academic, 2006.
Taylor, Justin. "Carson on the Gospel and Social Action." *TGC Blogs* (August 6, 2009). https://www.thegospelcoalition.org/blogs/justin-taylor/carson-on-gospel-and-social-action/.

BIBLIOGRAPHY

Tiénou, Tite. "The Church in African Theology." In *Biblical Interpretation and the Church: Text and Context*, edited by D.A. Carson, 151–65. Nashville: Thomas Nelson, 1984.

Tillich, Paul. *Christianity and the Encounter of the World Religions*. New York: Columbia University Press, 1963.

Tippett, Alan R. "Polygamy as a Missionary Problem: The Anthropological Issues." *Practical Anthropology* (March–April 1970) 75–79.

Tizon, F. Albert. "Remembering the Missionary Moratorium Debate: Toward a Missiology of Social Transformation in a Postcolonial Context." *Covenant Quarterly* 62 (February 2004) 13–34.

———. *Whole and Reconciled: Gospel, Church, and Mission in a Fractured World*. Grand Rapids: Baker Academic, 2018.

Toynbee, Arnold. *Christianity Among the Religions of the World*. New York: Charles Scribner's Sons, 1957.

Troeltsch, Ernst. "The Place of Christianity Among World Religions." In *Christianity and Other Religions: Selected Readings*, edited by John Hick and Brian Hebblethwaite, 11–31. London: Fount, 1980.

Van Rheenen, Gailyn. *Missions: Biblical Foundations and Contemporary Strategies*. Grand Rapids: Zondervan, 1996.

Visser't Hooft, W.A. *No Other Name: The Choice Between Syncretism and Christian Universalism*. Philadelphia: Westminster, 1963.

Vlach, Michael J. "Non-Typological Future-Mass-Conversion View." In *Three Views on Israel and the Church: Perspectives on Romans 9–11*, edited by Jared Compton and Andrew David Naselli, 21–74. Grand Rapids: Kregel Academic, 2018.

Walls, Andrew F. *The Missionary Movement in Christian History: Studies in the Transmission of Faith*. Maryknoll, NY: Orbis, 1996.

Wang, Wendy. "The Decline in Church Attendance in COVID America." *Institute for Family Studies* (January 20, 2022). https://ifstudies.org/blog/the-decline-in-church-attendance-in-covid-america.

Ware, Bruce A. "The New Covenant and People(s) of God." In *Dispensationalism, Israel and the Church*, edited by Craig A. Blaising and Darrell L. Bock, 68–97. Grand Rapids: Zondervan, 1992.

Weber, Jeremy. "God in Gaza." *Christianity Today* (February 10, 2009). https://www.christianitytoday.com/ct/2009/march/1.13.html.

Woodbury, J. Dudley, ed. *From Seed to Fruit: Global Trends, Fruitful Practices, and Emerging Issues Among Muslims*. 2nd ed. Pasadena, CA: William Carey, 2011.

Woodbury, J. Dudley, and Russell G. Shubin. "Why I Chose Jesus." *Mission Frontiers* (March 2001) 28–33. https://www.missionfrontiers.org/issue/article/muslims-tell...-why-i-chose-jesus.

Woudstra, Marten H. "Israel and the Church: A Case for Continuity." In *Continuity and Discontinuity: Perspectives on the Relationship Between the Old and the New Testaments*, edited by John S. Feinberg, 221–38. Wheaton, IL: Crossway, 1988.

BIBLIOGRAPHY

Wright, Christopher J. H. "Participatory Mission: The Mission of God's People Revealed in the Whole Bible Story." In *Four Views of the Church's Mission*, edited by Jason S. Sexton, 63–91. Grand Rapids: Zondervan, 2017.

Wright, N. T. *Surprised By Hope: Rethinking Heaven, the Resurrection, and the Mission of the Church*. New York: Harper One, 2008.

———. *What Saint Paul Really Said: Was Paul of Tarsus the Real Founder of Christianity?* Grand Rapids: Eerdmans, 1997.

Young, Lionel F. "How White Rule Ended in Missions." *Christianity Today* (December 13, 2021). https://www.christianitytoday.com/ct/2022/january-february/white-rule-ended-in-world-missions-lionel-young.html.

Zurlo Gina A., and Todd M. Johnson. "Is Christianity Shrinking or Shifting?" *Lausanne Global Analysis* 10 (March 2021). https://lausanne.org/lga-01/is-christianity-shrinking-or-shifting.